SOFTBALL
Concepts for Coaches and Teachers

Billie J. Jones
Florida State University

Mary Jo Murray
Northeast Missouri State University

wcb

Wm. C. Brown Company Publishers
Dubuque, Iowa 52001

c. 2

Contents

Part IV.
The Organization

Preface

We feel there is a great need for a well conceived and detailed text on the rapidly growing and popular sport of softball in both its forms—slow pitch and fast pitch. We hope that this book will contribute to the knowledge and skill of the players through increasing the knowlege and skill of their coaches and teachers.

We have divided our material into four distinct sections convering: I. *Basic information* including the history of the sport, the similarities and differences in fast and slow pitch play, the equipment, and the basic skills; II. *Offensive strategies* of batting and baserunning; III. *Defensive strategies* including position play in the infield and outfield and total defense; IV. *Organizational information* concerning the details of conditioning, coaching, and teaching.

We have tried to create an innovative structure within the body of our text, and we feel the format used for Chapters 4-10 may need some explanation to be clearly followed and utilized fully. Within each chapter we have listed the important information by rather broad concepts and then specified the key teaching/coaching points in very concrete terms to clarify each concept. Following each key point, we have given the appropriate biomechanical or strategical reason for suggesting a particular style in execution. We feel this is a real strength to be used in teaching the "whys" as well as the "hows" of each skill. We have concluded each section with teaching/learning tips and drills for further practice and a review that can be adapted by a teacher/coach to meet his particular situation and group.

We have tried to incorporate clear and accurate photographs and diagrams throughout the text to help clarify and illustrate the factual information visually. These can also be used as teaching aids.

Please note that all instructions are for righthanded players. Note also that we use the generic terms "he" and "man" to refer to persons of either gender. We have not specified in the text whether the material applies to slow pitch, fast pitch, or both games. We have assumed that the users of this book are aware of the major differences between the two games, which are discussed in Chapter 2.

We hope that you, the reader, will find our conceptual approach to softball factual, functional and practical!

Billie J. Jones
Mary Jo Murray

Acknowledgments

We owe a debt of thanks to those who helped make this endeavor possible:

. . . Our photographer, Mickey Adair
. . . Our illustrator, Hilda Dawson
. . . Our willing subjects

Jerry Steiger and his daughters Brenda, Kathy, and Sissy
Dr. Peter W. Everett
Florida State students Laura Davis, Diane Lawrence, Charlotte Martin and Wayne P. Richardson
Former Florida State students Liz Collins and Jo Anne Graf
Anthony Battle
Players from Jacksonville and Tallahassee teams, Sylvia Cross, Karin McGrath, Rose Ann Smith, Betty Stansel, and Dorothy Stansel.

. . . Teachers, coaches, students, and players too numerous to name.

A particular debt is owed to our families and friends who have supported us in our sports participation and in our writing endeavor.

BJJ

MJM

Part I
The Overview

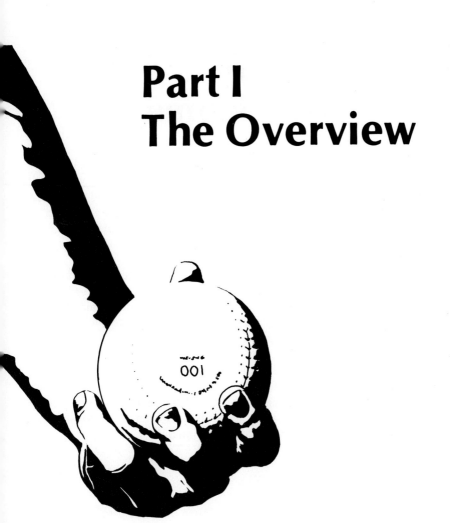

Chapter 1

History and Development

Ball games of one type or another have been played for thousands of years. However, the game of softball is a relatively young ball game if one considers being "born" within the last one hundred years to be young. A descendant of baseball and an outgrowth of a combination of games, softball had its start at the Farragut Boat Club in Chicago, Illinois, in 1887 where players used a boxing glove for a ball and a broom for a bat to play the game of "indoor baseball."

George W. Hancock, a recognized leader in the development of the new game, devised rules and provided a ball larger and softer than a baseball and a bat with a relatively small head. The indoor game became very popular because it could by played in a rather small area, was inexpensive, and offered a competitive experience.

Initially the game was played in the gymnasiums of colleges and universities, Young Mens Christian Associations (YMCA), and the Turnvereins, but the players soon moved outside to the playgrounds. Each community devised its own rules, and variations of the game were played under such names as Diamond Ball, Indoor Ball, Kitten Ball, Mush Ball, Playground Ball, Pumpkin Ball, and Recreation Ball.

The Early Years

Minneapolis, Minnesota, was the home of the first softball league, organized in 1900. League play was organized in other cities as well, but rapid growth did not occur until the "Roaring Twenties" when leagues and inter-city competition developed rapidly. It was during this period of time, in 1926, that the game acquired the present name, softball. Walter K. Hakanson, of the Denver YMCA, is given credit for naming it. The following year, 1927, the American Physical Education Association (APEA) adopted softball rules for girls and women that were devised by Gladys E. Palmer.

Interest grew to the extent that those who had true concern for the game and its participants feared that certain promoters would exploit anyone and anything associated with softball. There was also some confusion because there were innumerable sets of rules with varied interpretations. In 1932 a group of interested and concerned representatives from recreation, physical education, industrial recreation, and national agencies, as well as national promoters, met in Chicago and formed a Joint Rules Committee (JRC) in order to standardize the rules and begin national unity.

The Amateur Softball Association of America (ASA) was organized the next year, 1933, in a further attempt to satisfy the need to unify competition nationally. This need for unification was fully realized when a National Tournament was held at the Chicago World's Fair, Century of Progress Exposition, in the same year. Approximately twenty teams entered and there were about as many different sets of rules as there were teams. They played slow pitch and fast pitch, used different sized balls (twelve inches to seventeen inches in circumference), pitched from varying distances, and had dissimilar distances between bases. In spite of all the differences two national champions emerged—The Great Northerns (women) and the J.L. Boosters (men).

Post-national Organization

The year after the ASA was organized, 1934, the JRC and the sports equipment manufacturers, then the leading publishers of rules, reached an agreement whereby any rules that were published would be in accordance with the official rules authorized by the JRC. The official rules included many variations of the game and this was very evident in the 1937 published rules for girls and women.[1] See chart on page 4.

Softball became known as the "depression" sport as the game flourished in the 1930s. Growth slowed in the United States during World War II, the early 1940s, but flourished in other countries as American servicemen played the game wherever they were stationed and introduced softball to local populations throughout the world. Meantime, the JRC expanded its territory outside the boundaries of the states and changed its name to International Joint Rules Committee on Softball (IJRC).

In the early 1950s a different type of softball game was gaining

---

1. *Outdoor Baseball Rules for Girls and Women.* Supplement to *Official Baseball Guide for Girls and Women.* Spaulding Athletic Library no. 121 R, 1937, p. 6.

Size of Dia-mond (each side)	Pitching Distance	Distance Across Diamond*	Size of Ball	Type of Pitching
1. 35 feet ...	30 feet	49 1/2 feet	14 inch	underhand
2. 45 feet ...	37 feet 8 1/2 inches	63 feet	12 inch	underhand
3. 60 feet ...	37 feet 8 1/2 inches**	84 feet 9 inches	12 inch	over or underhand
4. 65 feet ...	40 feet	92 feet	12 or 9 inch play-ground ball	overhand

*From home to second base and from first base to third base.
**Or 33 feet for younger girls.

popularity, or perhaps an old variation continued to be played. This was slow pitch softball, and it became so popular in such a short time that a national tournament for men was held in 1953. Shields Contractors of Kentucky was the first National Slow Pitch Champion and in 1957 Dana Gardens, a team from Ohio, became the first Women's National Slow Pitch Champion.

Interest in the slow pitch game led to another national governing body being organized. The United States Slo-Pitch Softball Association (USSSA), with headquarters in Petersburg, Virginia, was formed in 1968 and is concerned only with the slow pitch softball game. The ASA, with headquarters in Oklahoma City, Oklahoma, continues to govern fast pitch as well as slow pitch play. The two sets of rules authorized by the two associations are similar but not identical.

Levels of Participation

"You've Come a Long Way, Baby" could be aptly applied to this game. From its beginning as a team sport less than a century ago the game has changed from one of varied names, many different rules, and few participants to one with a common name, unified rules, and the largest participation team sport in the United States. Over seventeen million people play on organized teams and another nine million play in pick-up games on sandlots, in backyards, and in recreational areas. Thirty-six million are playing in other countries.[2]

2. Correspondence with Dave Hill, ASA Public Relations Director, Oklahoma City, Oklahoma. 1976.

The game is for everyone, so it seems, regardless of age, interest level, or skill level. Tournaments abound. There are school tournaments, public recreation tournaments, armed forces tournaments, industrial league tournaments, church tournaments, and college tournaments, to name a few. In 1976 the ASA crowned twenty-one national champions while the USSSA crowned an almost equal number. In addition, State High School Activity Associations (HSAA) and the National Association for Girls and Womens Sports (NAGWS) supervised regular play and competition usually for girls, as boys typically compete in baseball. Collegiate level competition, again primarily for women, is available both for fast pitch and slow pitch. The National Fast Pitch Tournament, first played at John F. Kennedy College was conducted for several years before the first National Slow Pitch Tournament was held at Florida State University in 1976.

There are also international levels of competition. The Women's World Fast Pitch Tournament is held every four years. The first one, played in Australia in 1965, was won by the host team. The United States hosted the tournament in 1974 and won the championship and in 1978, this international event will be played in Canada. The United States team may have difficulty defending its title because many top players are now members of the International Women's Professional Softball League (IWPS).

The men began their World Tournament play in 1966, in Mexico City. Ten years later, 1976, there were three world champions—United States, New Zealand, and Canada—as rain halted the finals being played in New Zealand. These games are also held every four years, and Seattle, Washington, will be the site of the 1980 championships.

Softball is not as yet an Olympic sport but in 1967 the International Olympic Committee (IOC) recognized the International Softball Federation (ISF) and this is considered to be one of the first steps in becoming a part of the Olympic games. Softball is now played in almost fifty countries and is part of the Asian Games, Central American-Caribbean Games, and South Pacific Games, and it is scheduled to be a part of the 1979 Pan American Games.

Although softball has remained an amateur sport for most players, in 1976 the International Women's Professional Softball League (IWPS) was organized. Ten teams, divided into an Eastern League and a Western League, played an ambitious 120 game schedule of fast pitch ball. A World Series ended the season in September with the Eastern League champion Falcons using a roster filled with members of the 1976 ASA Fast Pitch Champions, Raybestos Brakettes, taking the first four games and becoming the winners of the first World Series of the Women's Professional Softball League. The late Philip K. Wrigley, owner of the Chicago Cubs professional baseball team, was a leader in organizing the women's American

Chapter 2

The Two Games

Softball is fun to play; otherwise, the millions of participants would choose to engage in a different game. The two games, fast pitch and slow pitch, are challenging and thrilling to play and exciting to watch. Basically, they are very much alike; the major differences, as the names imply, are found in the velocity and trajectory of the pitch. The ball is always pitched underhanded, but it may be lobbed across the plate in a high arch or go past the batter traveling eighty miles an hour. In both games offensive strategies are centered around getting on base and scoring runs while the defense maneuvers to prevent this.

Players in both ASA games travel sixty-foot base paths and sixty-five feet in USSSA games. The pitching distances are forty-six feet for all games except women's fast pitch in which the distance is forty feet. Official games are seven innings long; the equipment is the same, although in some slow pitch games a sixteen-inch ball is used.

Generally, the playing rules are identical; however, something has to be different if the score of a slow pitch game can be as high as 60-30 while the total runs scored in a fast pitch game is seldom over 10. A .600 batting average is fairly common in slow pitch play and a rarity in fast pitch leagues. Few, if any, players are struck out by a slow pitch pitcher while two out of three batters may go down swinging in a fast pitch game.

Differences are attributed to the pitching rules, as the fast pitch game was modified to shift the emphasis from pitching to hitting and fielding. In the slow pitch game the ball must be pitched at a moderate speed or slower with a perceptible arch. From the time the ball leaves the pitcher's hand until it crosses home plate it must travel in an arch of at least three feet and no greater than twelve feet. (Fig. 2.1)

Because of this style of pitching some rule changes were necessary. The strike zone had to be enlarged as it would be extremely difficult for a

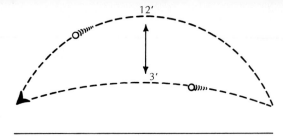

Fig. 2.1 Minimum and maximum heights of the pitching arc.

high arched ball to cross home plate between the batter's arm pits and the tops of the knees. Stealing was eliminated since it would not be difficult to advance to another base on a slowly pitched ball. Hit batsmen cannot take first base because anyone should be able to avoid being hit by a slowly moving ball.

As the ball is usually hit by the batter, and those batters with power hit home runs, fences had to be moved back. To encourage hitting, and since the ball is easily hit, bunting was disallowed. This rule change altered the strategies because squeeze plays, bunting to move a player to another base, and bunting to get on base were eliminated. Catchers are not required to wear protective equipment, though they should be encouraged to do so, as the danger of being hit by a pitched ball or a foul ball is not great.

Slow pitch is a hitter's game; very few players strike out or are awarded a walk. Ten players are placed on the field to reduce the chances of the batter hitting safely. The tenth player, a shortfielder, may play in the infield or outfield but is usually stationed in the outfield. (Fig. 2.2) This hitting factor often generates more team participation because fast pitch games frequently become dominated by the pitcher and catcher, and, if the batters strike out or fail to hit the ball well, defensive players have very little to do for seven innings.

More players participate in slow pitch games than in fast pitch ones. About twenty-five years after this new game emerged approximately eighty-two percent of the softball played in the United States was slow pitch softball.[1] During this time the game evolved from one for the "older" players and the younger ones who were not "good enough" to play fast pitch to an exciting game that is slow in name only.

One reason for the emphasis away from fast pitch is the lack of good pitchers. The ability to pitch a fast ball has not been developed in young players. This may change in the near future as pitchers are now being

1. Correspondence with Dave Hill, ASA Public Relations Director, Oklahoma City, Oklahoma, 1976.

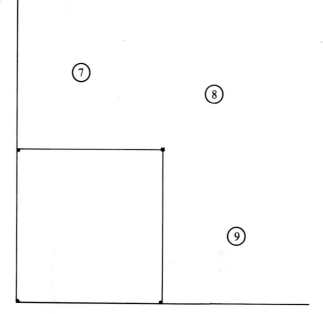

Fig. 2.2a Outfield for a fast pitch game.

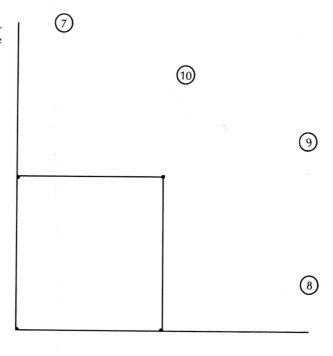

Fig. 2.2b Fourth outfielder added for the slow pitch game.

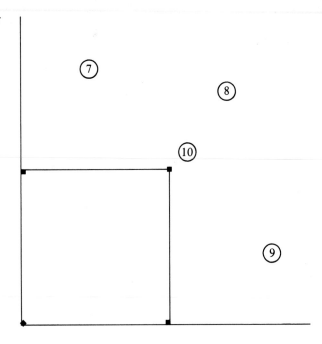

Fig. 2.2c Tenth player as the fifth infielder.

developed in the leagues for young players, both boys and girls, and ASA sponsors national tournaments for those thirteen years of age and older. This could possibly increase the interest in the fast pitch game.

Playing skills are essential for both games. One needs to be able to catch, throw, field, run, and bat and, the more proficient one becomes the better the games are played. Skill is a factor but the level of skill does not have to be high—anyone can play!

Major ASA Rule Difference

Rule	Fast Pitch	Slow Pitch
Playing Field		
Foul lines	225'	250' (F), 275' (M)
Pitching distance	40' (F), 46' (M)	46'
Players	9	10
Equipment		
Mask	Required	Recommended
Chest protector	Required	Recommended
Pitching		
Velocity	Unlimited	Moderate or slower
Trajectory	Unlimited	3'-12' arch
Windup	Optional	Illegal
Strike zone	Between arm pits and tops of knees	Between highest shoulder and knees
Batting		
Bunting	Legal	Illegal
Chopping	Legal	Illegal
Hit by pitch	Take base	Ball or strike
Walk	Four balls	Four balls or told to take base
Three strikes	Out only if less than 2 outs and runner on first	Out
Baserunning		
Stealing	Legal	Illegal
Leaving base	Ball leaves pitcher's hand	Ball crosses plate or hit by batter

Chapter 3

Equipment

Equipment is a necessary part of the game. The quality, quantity, and care of merchandise are extremely important and careful planning should be made regarding its selection and purchase. Problems relating to purchase and care are numerous and vary with the situation, but some can be alleviated by adhering to a few basic principles.

Purchasing Equipment

Check the inventory to know the needs, review the rules and regulations for equipment limitations and restrictions, and determine the amount of money that has been allotted for the season. Be aware of the quality of the merchandise and buy the best possible as this will be less expensive over an extended period of time. Quality items will usually be well-proportioned and fit better; more durable and last for a greater number of seasons; more dependable regarding color, shape, and size; better made and require less care; and safer and afford better protection.

Test equipment before making large purchases. Ask the company to send a sample; most will be happy to furnish one. Be open to new ideas and styles but do not sacrifice quality for novelty. Read all specifics given about the item to be familiar with the material, design, utility, cost of maintenance, safety factors in protective equipment, and comparative costs.

Know your supply source. Buy from reputable firms, preferably local firms if the quality, cost, and services are equal. It is easier to deal with someone nearby than someone who is many miles away. Buy in quantity, and consider purchasing standardized merchandise from open stock as this can be more economical. Choose items that can be easily maintained without utilizing special tools and special people.

Balls

Balls come in different sizes (9 inch, 12 inch, 14 inch, and 16 inch), with different centers (rubber, cork, and/or kapok), and enclosed in different covers (rubber, fleece, leather). One may buy a soft softball, an indoor ball, an outdoor ball, a restricted flight ball, an official slow pitch ball, or an official fast pitch ball. Make sure that the right ball is bought for the game that is to be played and that it has smooth, straight seams. Soft fleece balls are available for indoor use and rubber covered balls are good for class use as they are less expensive, softer, and will stand a greater amount of abuse before losing the cover or shape.

Bats

Wooden bats, usually made of ash, are still being used as they are less expensive initially and some prefer to hit with them, but they are being replaced rapidly by aluminum ones. An aluminum bat may cost more, possibly three times the cost of a wooden one, but it will last indefinitely and may give a team a psychological advantage.

Be cognizant of the rules concerning the length, weight, grip, and construction before buying, as well as the ages and sizes of the players who will be using the bat. Bats come in different lengths, 27 inches to 34 inches, and different weights, 22 ounces to 34 ounces. The length may be stamped on the bat but neither the weight nor the length is marked on many bats so you may want to weigh and measure before buying. Different weight bats are needed for different situations, especially in fast pitch games where one may choose to use a heavy bat against a slower pitcher and a lighter bat against a faster pitcher. If a long bat is used a batter may want to go with a lighter weight in order to get the bat around to meet the ball. If a shorter bat is used one may prefer to use a heavier weight, which will increase the force produced.

Gloves and Mitts

These items are strictly personal equipment and should be bought for a specific player who intends to play a specific position. Often players choose to buy baseball gloves or mitts even though softball items can be purchased. Baseball gloves are more readily available and many players seem to think that they are generally more durable and usable. Leather, tanned hide, is used in making the better ones. There are varying grades of leather and the higher the grade, the higher the price. The higher grade leather glove will be more pliable and durable.

There are two-fingered, three-fingered, and four-fingered styles of gloves. Many outfielders prefer a long-fingered glove with considerable webbing, lacing, and a deep pocket. This type will give a longer reach, which is often needed to cover the vast amount of outfield territory, and good pocket, which is necessary for catching the hard-to-get-to balls. An infielder may choose to buy a glove with shorter fingers and less webbing as infielders have less territory to cover and must get the ball out of the pocket and across the diamond very quickly. However, the amount of webbing is an indication of the amount of care that went into the manufacture. Generally, the more webbing, the longer the life of the glove. Expensive gloves have webbing, not a piece of leather, between the thumb and first finger.

Mitts come in two basic styles—catcher's mitt and first baseman's mitt. The first baseman's mitt can be a trapper, snare, openface, or clutch model and is used by many catchers as it gives a longer reach and more catching space than a catcher's mitt. They both confine the four fingers into one section, with the thumb remaining separate, but the catcher's mitt is more circular and more heavily padded.

All-purpose sports gloves, comparable to golf gloves, are worn by many players. If only one is worn while batting it is usually placed on the hand nearest the end of the bat. Two are sometimes worn and not only do they help in gripping the bat but also protect the hands during slides. The fast pitch catcher may wear one for additional protection under the mitt.

Protective Equipment

Caps

This item is considered as protective equipment by many players and coaches because a cap can shield the eyes from the sun and also keep hair out of one's eyes. Caps, required to be worn by all players in USSSA leagues and by the men in ASA leagues, should be ordered by the actual size. The style is not regulated so many players wear a type of sun visor instead of the regular "baseball" cap. It is stated in the rules that a cap is part of the uniform and all must wear the same color and style. Also, if one member of the team wears one, all must wear one.

Chest Protectors

A catcher in a fast pitch game is required to wear a chest protector, and all catchers should be encouraged to do so. This is particularly true in a class situation and in games with younger players as they may have less playing experience and have not developed the proper techniques. Leagues may make ground rules covering the wearing of this protective equipment even though the national slow pitch rules (ASA) do not require this. Some ladies' models have cup-shaped breast protectors but they are not of great value as this area should be protected by the mitt. Short style body protectors worn by little leaguers could be worn by the female or young male.

Masks

The wearing of a mask is required when playing fast pitch but optional, though recommended, in a slow pitch game. Ground rules may require that a mask be worn and players should be encouraged to wear one to protect the face from foul tips. This area is not as easily protected by the mitt as is the chest area. Those purchased should be light in weight, allow a wide range of visibility but protect the face, and be comfortable to the catcher. An aluminum-framed mask gives great protection, especially for those wearing glasses, but limits overall visibility. Those framed with wire are lighter and give a greater visibility range but do not give the overall protection that is given by one with an aluminum frame.

Shoes

Read the rules before buying shoes. The primary concern is with the cleat that may be worn. The size is regulated and some leagues prohibit the use of metal cleats. Most of the shoes worn by the softball players have leather or canvas uppers. Leather gives the foot more support and will last longer but is more expensive. Shoes worn by little league, soccer, and field hockey players work quite well in a softball game. A fast pitcher should wear a metal toe plate on the shoe that is used to push off the pitcher's plate to prevent the toe of the shoe from wearing out.

Socks

The softball hose are usually tube socks, without a toe or heel, that are worn over another pair(s) of socks. These are usually made of synthetic material (orlon, nylon, etc.) or a blend of materials. They are colorful, fit neatly, feel comfortable, and are long wearing. These knee socks come to just below the knee and if knickers are worn, they fit underneath the pants. They afford some protection against abrasions and may help prevent muscle cramps by keeping "warmed-up" legs warm.

The basic sock, the one worn inside the shoe, can be made of almost any material, but wool socks and cotton socks absorb perspiration more readily than those made of synthetic materials. Wool socks may be too bulky to wear so that cotton socks or ones that are a combination of materials are worn. They also come in a variety of colors; however, white may be the best choice as the color may bleed when wet and the dye is a potential blister infector. Socks should be worn to protect the feet, though there is no rule to this effect, and the wearing of two pair will afford more protection against blisters.

Uniforms

Read the rules before buying uniforms. The style will be a matter of personal choice—the shirt may be long-sleeved, short-sleeved or sleeveless; the neckline may have a collar or be collarless, have a v-neck, round neck, or crew neck; the shirttail may be long and hemmed or short and ribbed. The pants may be short shorts, bermudas, jamaicas, knickers, or full length. One can tell by observation which styles give more protection, but one should also be concerned with freedom of movement and comfort. A team would like to make a good appearance on the field so fit, color, and style are serious considerations.

After selecting the style, consider the type of material. Keep the following in mind when buying uniforms.

1. Colorfast sew-on numerals give the best service but are more expensive.
2. Screen-printed markings give a flat appearance and tend to lose some color with each laundering but, if properly applied, should give satisfactory service for the life of the garment.
3. Flock markings give a dimensional effect similar to sew-on letters but may crack and lose some flocking with each laundering; however, if properly applied, they should give satisfactory service for the life of the garment.
4. Colors and stripes increase the chances that colors will bleed and run.
5. Even though there is a tendency to shrink with laundering, knitwear garments can be satisfactory if the manufacturer has used a shrink control process and cut the garment properly.
6. Garments—complete with fabric, proper colors, and proper trim—should be tested before a large purchase is made.[1]

Care of Equipment

Equipment will not last forever but proper care can increase the longevity of the item. Do not continue to use an item when it has deteriorated to the point that a player's safety is endangered by using it, but do not throw items away that could be repaired and used over a longer period of time. When merchandise is received all items should be marked.

---

1. American Institute of Laundering, Joliet, Illinois

This will identify ownership, make checking-out and checking-in of items more efficient, and aid in determining the life span of a specific item.

When marking, be careful in the selection of the marking instrument to be used and where the item is to be marked. Some inks may fade into the uniforms when laundered; any dark ink on dark material cannot be easily located. The mark should be located in an area that can be quickly spotted but not mar the appearance or be distracting to the performer. Most fabrics can be marked with a felt tip pen or stencil. Use an indelible pencil, rubber stamp, or stencil on leather or rubber materials. A leather burning pen can be used to mark a leather item that is not inflated.

Cleaning

READ the instructions attached to the item very carefully. Take an item and clean it according to the instructions and then observe the results for any marked changed such as shrinkage, fading, bleeding of colors, and wrinkling. Clean the item before the dirt or stain has had time to set in. If the individual player is to be responsible for items that are checked out, inform each of the proper use and care. A printed sheet could be given to individuals as an item is checked out. Following general principles when laundering or cleaning will save money by protecting the life of the item.

Uniforms
1. Wash white items alone.
2. Wash different colored items separately—do not mix colors.
3. Wash bright colors in luke warm water, 110° to 120° F., to set the color.
4. Use bleach only on cotton or white items.
5. Rinse in water the same temperature as the wash water.
6. Dry clean items containing wool as well as the all woolen ones.
7. Use rust proof hangers for hang drying.
8. Tumble dry at a low temperature to reduce shrinkage.

Leather
1. Use vaseline or petroleum jelly to soften if the item is dry.
2. Use water to stiffen the leather if the item is limp or too flexible.
3. Clean with a hand brush, a little saddle soap, and a little water.
4. Dry at room temperature.
5. Care for shoes by:
    a. Using shoe trees or paper stuffed inside to retain shape.
    b. Oiling the outside (waterproof oil can give added protection).
    c. Polishing.
    d. Spraying the inside with a disinfectant.

      e.   Checking, and replacing if necessary, innersoles, laces, and cleats.

Canvas
1. Wash in lukewarm water with a mild soap.
2. Drip dry.

Rubber
1. Clean with soap and water.
2. Wipe dry.

Wood
1. Wipe off dirt.
2. Wipe with a light oil.

Aluminum
1. Wipe off dirt.
2. Wipe dry with a clean cloth.

Repair

Sew up rips and tears in uniforms immediately. A machine stitch will be stronger than a hand stitch. Zippers can be replaced easily as can buttons, belt loops, elastic bands, and hems. Reweb gloves and resew loose stitches. If a bat breaks, throw it away; at least do not use it in practice or game situations. All equipment exposed to moisture should be wiped dry at once.

Storage

Clean, repair, and mark the equipment before storing it in a dry, cool, and well-ventilated area. Place paper on shoe trees in shoes before storing in a plastic bag. Balls, both rubber and leather, should be placed in the original box. Bats, both wooden and aluminum, should be stored in the original carton and stacked on the shelf or placed upright in a storage bin or bat rack. Place the uniforms on rust proof hangers in a wardrobe cabinet or on garment racks. If there is no hanging space, fold and place on shelves or in plastic containers. Gloves and mitts should be stored with a ball molded in the pocket.

Fitting

To ensure a good fit, take the player's measurements before placing an order. When measuring use a cloth or plastic tape measure and pull it snugly but not so tightly that the skin is "indented." Take the measurements over what will be worn underneath the garment while the player stands with arms at his sides, except when the arm length is checked. Place the tape around the:

Chest	Males. Under the arms and over the shoulder blades. Females. Over the largest part of the breasts. (read tape at center of front or back)
Waist	At the smallest part of the trunk, the waistline. (read tape from the side)
Hips	At the largest part of the buttocks (read tape from the side)
Inseam	From the crotch to the top of the heel of the shoe. (full length pants) (read tape at the heel)
Outseam	From the waist (at the side) line to the top of the heel of the shoe. (read tape at heel)
Head	Across the forehead about 1 1/2 inches above the eyebrows and around the largest part of the head.
Arm	From the center of the back, over the elbow to the wrist to the wrist joint at the back of the hand. Flex the elbow at an approximate 45° angle and hold the upper arm parallel with the floor. (read the tape at the wrist)

Carefully read the manufacturer's guide to sizes. Generally, the shirts and pants are made to actual size. If a player wants a loose fitting uniform, order the next size; if a player is exceptionally tall, order extra long lengths. Women who are exceptionally difficult to fit may choose to order a man's or boy's uniform. A man may need to order a boy's size or a boy may order a man's uniform.

If uniforms cannot be ordered for the individual and must be ordered in bulk, the general rule is to order more of the "average" sizes than large or small sizes, e.g., if eighteen are ordered, buy eight average, four small, four large, and two extra large ones. Purchasing standard sizes, recommended by the manufacturer, may be more efficient than individual fittings and is a lot more practical. It takes time to measure individuals, and if you order one year for the team the next year the players may grow or the personnel change.

Warm-up jackets should be ordered at least a size larger than the actual measurement. Take into consideration what is to be worn underneath and also the jacket material. Two sizes larger is a general guide to buying. These should be very functional—shed water, keep one warm (a lining in a nylon jacket) and be comfortable—as well as attractive.

Glossary of Uniforms and Equipment Materials

Uniform Materials

Acetate A man-made fiber that looks and feels like silk and is highly resistant to wrinkling.

Acrylic A man-made fiber that is soft and has a tendency to retain pressed creases. It is highly resistant to sunlight, holds up well to repeated launderings, and resists wrinkling.

Combed A process in which all short fibers are combed out and impurities are eliminated giving extra strength, evenness, and fineness to cotton yarns.

Cotton A natural fiber making garments that are light, cool, and colorfast; when Sanforized shrinkage is not a problem.

Cut The indication of the number of threads running both ways in an inch of material, i.e., fifteen cut would have fifteen threads running in each direction in one square inch.

Dacron A polyester fiber that requires minumum care as it has excellent resilience and high tensile strength and is highly resistant to abrasions, chemical bleaches, wrinkling, and mildew. The fiber blends well with cotton and various man-made fibers.

Denier The size of yarn used in weaving or knitting; the higher the yarn number, the finer the yarn will be. (14 denier yarn would have a smaller diameter than 12 denier yarn).

Durene The highest grade cotton material that is strong, smooth, durable, and stronger wet than when dry. It maintains its good looks, takes dye, requires no special care, is easy to wash, sheds dirt, dries fast, and absorbs and evaporates moisture.

Fortrel The trademark for a polyester fiber that has good color fastness, excellent wash and wear qualities, and good strength but may pill in certain constructions faster than ordinary cottons and most synthetics.

Gabardine A highly woven cotton or rayon fabric that is durable, of medium weight, and has many fine qualities of the material of which it is made.

Gabracord	An all-cotton twill weave of medium quality.
Helenca Yarn	A type of viscose rayon that is wool-like but is better in regard to resistance to shrinkage; basically not damaged by alkalies.
Jockey Satin	A fine woven cotton back and rayon front material that is easy to work with, light in weight, colorful, and of average durability.
Kodel IV (also II, S, III)	A wash and wear synthetic fiber with build-in optical brightener that is claimed to be resistant to washing and dry cleaning. May become discolored because of soil pick up or color pick up in laundering but retains creases and pleats, has excellent resilience, and requires minimum care.
Knitted Stretch	A fabric constructed by knitting stretch yarns. It does not stretch out of shape as easily as regular knitted fabrics and has greater holding power.
Multi-ply	The twisting together of two or more yarns giving greater strength and evenness to materials.
Nylon	A synthetic yarn that has good strength, durability, and sheen; it is easily laundered, quick drying, lightweight, and transparent; and it has low moisture-absorbing and mildew properties. It does not dye well.
Nylon Durene	A synthetic fabric, nylon on the outside and durene on the inside, that is very good but expensive. It looks like nylon and has the strength of nylon while possessing the softness and absorption power of durene.
Nylon Fleece	A fabric processed to look like brushed wool.
Nylon Satin	A smooth silky fabric with a flashy finish. It does not absorb moisture, requires considerable care, and is the most expensive of all satin cloth.
Nylon Twill	A most desirable, long-wearing material. It appears hard and shiny and is also known as nylon combat cloth.
Nystretch	An all-knit material of Helenca yarn that requires considerable care but is an excellent fitting material that stretches in all directions and is cool.
Orlon	A synthetic fiber that is highly resistant to sunlight and gases present in the air, soft, and used alone or in blends. It has dimensional stability and good drapability.
Polyester	A generic term for man-made fibers that are abrasion

	and crease resistant, quick drying, and strong. The material retains its shape and requires minimum care.
Rayon	A synthetic yarn that has a high sheen characteristic, dyes easily, and is stronger dry than when wet. It is often combined with other fabrics.
Rayon Satin	A material similar to jockey satin but with a lower sheen.
Spandex	An excellent fitting but expensive fabric that has high stretch potential, good recovery value, is strong and highly resistant to abrasions.
Staple	A length of thread after it is combed and carded—short, medium, or long. Long staple cotton is used in the more expensive garments.
Tackle Twill	A combination of materials, cotton on the inside and rayon on the outside, that have the strength and absorption qualities of both materials.
Twill Weave	A weave that makes fabrics closer in texture, heavier and stronger than ordinary weaves, and is generally more expensive.
Viscose	A viscous solution used in making cellulose fibers such as rayon.
Warp Mercerized	A process that results in materials being dyed more evenly, knitted more smoothly, and capable of absorbing and evaporating moisture faster than ordinary cotton yarns.
Wool	A natural fiber coming from sheep that is warm, durable, and absorbs moisture; but it can be scratchy, smell when wet, and shrink when drying.

Equipment Materials

Aluminum	A silver white metallic element that is light weight, malleable, not easily tarnished nor readily oxidized.
Bend	The best part of the animal's hide that is usually thick, firm, and relatively free of defects or scars and is used in making more expensive equipment.
Canvas	A closely woven, heavy material made from natural fibers—cotton, flax, or hemp. It is very strong and durable.
Cowhide	A heavy durable leather that has strength, thickness, and body and is used in gloves and soles of athletic footwear.
Felt	A matted or wrought cloth or fabric made of wool,

	wool and fur, or hair. It is an excellent shock and water absorber.
Horsehide	A material with high scuff-resistant qualities used in making balls, mitts, and gloves. It is inferior to cowhide or steerhide in qualities of strength, texture, and thickness.
Kangaroo	A material that is supple, tough, and several times thicker than the grain of other types of skin. It is seventeen times stronger than any other shoe leather, resists water, and will not peel or crack. Tiny holes in the skin permit the leather to breathe.
Kangaroo Blue-back	The kangaroo skin is made even more durable by the use of a special oil base tanning process.
Kangaroo Yellow-back	A stronger, softer leather than the blue-back that is used for athletic shoes exclusively.
Kangaroo Calf	An imitation kangaroo skin.
Kangaroo Horse	An imitation kangaroo skin.
Kangaroo Side	An imitation kangaroo skin.
Kapok	A material used in less expensive items as a shock absorber. Quilting prevents bunching up.
Petroleum Jelly	A petroleum derivative that is a semi-solid, transparent, gelatinous, oily, formless mass used as a lubricant and rust preventative.
Resilite	A synthetic rubber used in protective equipment.
Rubber	A very elastic, solid substance that is made from the milky juice of rubber trees.
Sheepskin	A hide that is thin and has a loose, spongy texture, scratches easily and is used in less expensive gloves and balls. It is not as strong or durable as the other skins or hides.

Chapter 4

Basic Skills

The basic skills—throwing, catching, and running—are not peculiar to the game of softball. These are used in countless games and activities and are taught (and hopefully learned) in the primary grades, or earlier, as children are capable of mastering highly complex motor skills. Regardless of the age or skill level, these fundamentals should be of primary interest to the teacher/coach and receive attention during instructional periods. (Fig. 4.1) One must become proficient to some degree in these in order to play the game.

Throwing

The overhand throw is probably the basic throw in softball but the type of throw—overhand, sidearm or underhand—will depend upon the

Fig. 4.1 Teach the basic skills.

play. An outfielder will need an overhand throw to return the ball to the infield while the infielder will often use an underhand whip or sidearm throw to get rid of the ball more quickly and have the ball travel a shorter distance. (Fig. 4.2a, b) An underhand toss is used by an infielder who is very near the baseman to receive the throw. (Fig. 4.2c)

Fig. 4.2a Preparing to throw overhand from the outfield.

Fig. 4.2b Preparing to throw sidearm from an infield position.

Fig. 4.2c Completing an underhand toss.

This skill, as are the other basic skills, is dependent upon the coordinated movement of the body. The body parts involved must be brought into action at the precise instant in order to make the most efficient and effective play. There are three stages involved—preparatory, throwing, and follow through.

CONCEPT: Correct use of the body when throwing will yield a more efficient throw.

Key Points: Preparatory Stage

1. Grip the ball by placing the ends of the first and second fingers across a seam, the third and fourth fingers at the side and the thumb underneath. (Fig. 4.3a) A young player or one with small hands may place three or four fingers across a seam. (Fig. 4.3b)

   Gains control of the ball; keeps it from "sailing"; and allows proper wrist action

2. Point the elbow away from the body as the arm begins to move back. (Fig. 4.4a)

Fig. 4.3a Adult's hand gripping the ball.   **Fig. 4.3b** Child's hand gripping the ball.

Allows the throwing arm to move farther rearward and then to be brought forward in a continous motion.

3. Place the body weight on the right foot as the trunk is rotated clockwise and the arm is brought back, with the elbow leading and the elbow and wrist flexed, until the ball is near ear level. (Fig. 4.4b)

    Increases the range of movement to increase the distance through which force can be developed.

4. Hyperextend the wrist; keep the elbow flexed and pointed away from the body.

    Makes use of longer, as well as more, levers.

5. Hold the left arm in front of the body and step forward on the left foot; point the left shoulder and foot toward the target.

    Increases the body's stability.

Key Points: Throwing Stage

1. Give a big push with the right leg as the hips, trunk, and shoulders rotate sharply counterclockwise and the weight shifts forward.

    Sets the body parts in motion in proper sequence to build power.

2. Lead with the elbow and keep it at a level lower than the ball as the arm, wrist, and hand come forward.

    Permits the greatest summation of forces.

3. Extend the arm; snap the hand forward; throw from the shoulder as the final impetus is given by the flexor muscles of the wrist and fingers; release the ball off the fingers. (Fig. 4.4c)

    Gains power from the use of the long lever and several levers as backspin is imparted to give direction to the flight.

Fig. 4.4a Bringing the ball back with the elbow pointing away from the body.

Fig. 4.4b Bringing the ball forward with the elbow leading and the wrist hyperextended.

Fig. 4.4c Releasing the ball.

Key Points: Follow Through Stage

1. Bring the arm forward and then downward across the body. (Fig. 4.5a)

   Ensures maximum control and power as the force is transferred to the ball.

2. Step with the right foot; use a reverse turn. (Fig. 4.5b)

   Adds force for longer throws.

Fig. 4.5a Following through after an overhand throw.

Fig. 4.5b Using a reverse turn follow through to gain additional power.

Catching

Catching a ball involves the same basic principles as breaking a fall—the arms absorb the force of the impact. The arms recoil to absorb the force of a falling body and they should recoil to absorb the force of a moving object, the ball. Gloves and mitts should be worn on the nonthrowing hand to make a larger catching area and to protect the hand from the force of impact. The hand should not be placed completely into the glove but just far enough to ensure good control. (Fig. 4.6) Some players elect to keep the index finger outside while others choose to place all digits inside. This is a matter of individual style and the type of glove being worn.

Fig. 4.6 Placing all fingers inside a glove.

CONCEPT: **Catching the ball correctly will result in fewer errors and injuries.**

Key Points:

1. Expect the ball; know what is to be done when it is caught; relax.

    Gives complete attention to catching.

2. Get in front of the ball and stand in a forward stride position.

   Stabilizes the body and establishes the best position for absorbing force of impact.

3. Direct the palms of the hand toward the ball (entire face of the glove faces the ball). If the ball is to be received high, hold the thumbs together and point the fingers upward; if the ball is received low, hold the little fingers together and point the fingers downward. (Fig. 4.7a-b)

   Gives a large target to control the ball and reduces the force of the impact.

4. Extend the arms toward the ball; keep the elbows slightly flexed.

   Makes contact as soon as possible and sets the arms to be shock absorbers.

5. Watch the ball into the glove and recoil the arms as soon as contact is made.

   Tracks the ball until contact is made and the force is absorbed.

6. Entrap the ball with the glove and close the throwing hand over it.

   Assures the catch and prepares for a quick throw.

Fig. 4.7a Preparing to catch a high throw by placing the glove square with the ball. The fingers of the right hand should also be pointed upward rather than toward the ball.

Fig. 4.7b Catching a low throw with the fingers pointing downward and the right hand getting ready to grip the ball to throw.

Fielding and Throwing

Field, grip, and throw the ball with rhythmic movement. There are no pauses among these steps but the motion should be a fluid one beginning with the first step toward the ball and continuing until the completion of the follow through.

CONCEPT: Proper execution of these skills will result in better defensive play.

Key Points: Fielding

1. Assume the ready position. Place the feet in a comfortable side stride position; flex the hips and knees; keep the back straight and at an approximate 45° angle with the hips; place the hands on the knees; and keep the eyes on the pitcher. (Fig. 4.8a)

   Establishes a resting but alert position.

2. Take the hands off the knees and hang them loosely between the legs as the weight is shifted forward and the eyes move from pitcher to batter. (Fig. 4.8b)

   Prepares for a quick start to move into position to field the ball.

Fig. 4.8a Ready position before the ball is pitched.

Fig. 4.8b Ready position as the ball is pitched.

3. Get in front of the ball.

   Establishes the most efficient position to field and then throw the ball.

4. Take the first step forward with either foot to meet a ball hit directly to you; stay low (keep the glove below the level of the ball) and watch the ball. If the ball is hit slightly to the right, take the first step on the right foot; if it is hit slightly to the left, take the first step on the left foot.

   Permits the shortest route to be taken to place the body in front of the ball.

5. Get in front of a ball that is hit farther to the right by turning on the right foot and crossing over with the left; turn on the left foot and cross over with the right to move left. (Fig. 4.9a, b, c, d)

   Permits the quickest movement to get in front of the ball.

Fig. 4.9a Turning on the right foot to move to the right to field a ground ball.

Fig. 4.9b Turning on the left foot to get in line with the ball.

a   b

Fig. 4.9c Turning on the left foot to move to the left to field a ground ball.

Fig. 4.9d Turning on the right foot to get in line with the ball. The fielder should have the glove down into position.

c   d

6. Move back at an approximate 45° angle to field a hard hit ball traveling far to either side.
   Gives more time to move in front of the ball.
7. Keep the feet comfortably spread, weight forward, knees and hips flexed, arms relaxed and hands well out in front of the feet. (Fig. 4.10a)
   Establishes a stable position and one that enables the fielder to reach the ball easily and quickly.
8. Square the face of the glove with the ball; keep the head down and watch the ball into the glove. As the ball is fielded, draw the arms back toward the belt line. (Fig. 4.10b, c)
   Yields a large target and permits an immediate throw

Fig. 4.10a Moving forward to field a ground ball keeping the glove low and the body in line with the ball.

Fig. 4.10b Squaring the face of the glove with the ball and using the right hand to ensure the catch and to be in position to begin the throw.

Fig. 4.10c Preparing to throw by quickly bringing the ball toward the waist.

9. Charge slowly moving ground balls; approach the slowly moving bouncing balls or ones that are stopped, from the right side. (Fig. 4.11)
   Permits arrival at the ball quickly and cuts down on the angle of the throw to first base.
10. Block the hard hit balls with the body if necessary.
    Keeps the ball in the infield and yields a chance to make a play on the runner.

Key Points: Gripping and Throwing

1. Fold the throwing hand over the ball to grip for the throw as it is caught in the glove; grip the same way for all throws, preferably on a seam.

Prepares for a quick, smooth movement from fielding to throwing.

2. Avoid taking extra steps in order to release the ball.

Gets the ball away more quickly.

3. Throw sidearm if there is not enough time to straighten up to make an overhand throw; flex the arm very slightly and keep it parallel with the ground.

Saves time between fielding and throwing.

4. Throw underhand for getting the ball a short distance; keep the body low and get power by using a full wrist snap.

Yields a quick throw to cover a short distance.

Running

Running is the one fundamental skill that is used offensively and defensively. This skill should be practiced as it should not be assumed that running comes naturally. Running can be taught, but it is often neglected.

The basic idea is to direct all effort into moving in one direction, generally forward. Motions, such as toeing out and swinging the arms across the body, which cause one to deviate from a straight line, should be avoided. There is a mechanically efficient way to run.

CONCEPT: Good running form contributes to defensive and offensive playing skills.

Key Points: (Fig. 4.12)

1. Hold the head up; focus the eyes ahead.

   Yields a complete view of the field—the ball, the defense, the runners, the coaches.

2. Use the arms; swing them freely from the shoulders—forward and backward (not across the body) and keep them close to the sides.

   Helps to propel the body and move it in a straight line.

3. Stay relaxed; close the hands loosely; swing the arms easily; and do not force the movements.

   Permits more movement using less energy.

5. Swing the legs freely and easily from the hips; point the toes straight ahead; land on the balls of the feet and touch the heels to the ground lightly.

   Propels the body in a straight line as the legs and feet are used as shock absorbers.

6. Push off from the balls of the feet and the toes; lift the knees.

   Produces power in one direction.

Fig. 4.12 Good running form.

Teaching/Learning Tips and Drills

1. To break in a new mitt put a "handful" of hot water in the pocket and rub it in. Catch hard thrown balls in the pocket. Oil lightly.

2. To break in a new glove put a handful of hot water into the pocket and rub it in. Place a softball in the pocket, wrap tightly and let it dry slowly. Oil lightly, castor oil is good, after it dries.

3. To practice watching the ball into the glove, the player should make a conscious effort to "read" the print or "count" the stitches on the ball as it comes into the glove. He should watch the white blend with the brown. The player can toss the ball to himself and catch it or receive throws from another player.

4. To practice catching and throwing, the players should be paired off or placed in groups of two or three, with each group getting a ball. As the players practice throwing and catching, the distance is gradually increased. If the players are inexperienced, they should begin by throwing short distances, about thirty feet, increasing the distance slowly. Have the flight of the ball vary—the height (chest high, knee high, head high), the velocity (slow, moderate, fast), and the direction (left or right). Throwing directions can be called out to ensure a variety in the throws. The overhand throw is the most widely used in a game and should be practiced by all players. (Fig. 4.13)

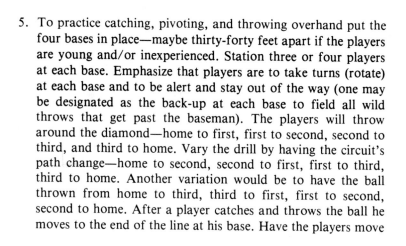

Fig. 4.13 Basic catching and throwing drill.

5. To practice catching, pivoting, and throwing overhand put the four bases in place—maybe thirty-forty feet apart if the players are young and/or inexperienced. Station three or four players at each base. Emphasize that players are to take turns (rotate) at each base and to be alert and stay out of the way (one may be designated as the back-up at each base to field all wild throws that get past the baseman). The players will throw around the diamond—home to first, first to second, second to third, and third to home. Vary the drill by having the circuit's path change—home to second, second to first, first to third, third to home. Another variation would be to have the ball thrown from home to third, third to first, first to second, second to home. After a player catches and throws the ball he moves to the end of the line at his base. Have the players move

Fig. 4.14 Catching and throwing drill using bases.

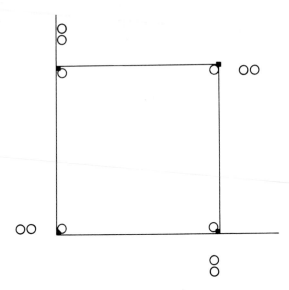

to another base, all rotate in a clockwise direction, after several circuits have been completed. (Fig. 4.14)

6. To practice catching a throw from an outfielder and then "relaying" it in to another infielder place the group in lines of three. Player "1" throws a fly ball to player "3" who catches the ball and throws it to player "2." Player "2" then turns and throws the ball to "1," completing the play. Rotate the positions after several plays and gradually increase the distance. (Fig. 4.15)

7. To practice keeping the body and glove low for fielding a ground ball, the player should touch the grass or dirt with the glove each time before fielding the ball.

8. To practice fielding the players should be placed in pairs. Two balls should be given to each pair. One player tosses a ground ball to the left or right of his partner who fields the ball quickly

Fig. 4.15 More advanced catching and throwing drill.

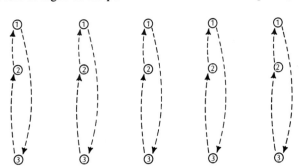

36 Basic Skills

and tosses it back in the air. As soon as the fielder has released the ball, the player tosses another grounder. Keep the pace brisk but not so fast that the fielder finds it impossible to field the balls. After twenty ground balls rotate positions. Vary the distance between the two and the type of throw the fielder is to use in returning the balls to the partner.

9. To practice fielding ground balls and throwing the players should be divided into groups. A designated player will throw ground balls—varying the speed and the path—to the other players in the group who field it and throw it back. Rotate duties and vary the distance. (If the players are placed in a straight line, less space is needed and it will be easier for beginning players to "take turns.") (Fig. 4.16a)

10. To practice fielding batted balls use drill 9 except add a fungo batter. Place the players so that there is a batter, a catcher, and fielders. Place the catcher on the right side of a righthanded batter and on the left side of a lefthanded batter. Fungo ten balls before rotating positions. Vary the distances and the type of ball that is hit. (Fig. 4.16b)

11. To practice fielding ground balls and then throwing use drill 5 but use a fungo batter to put the ball into play at the plate.

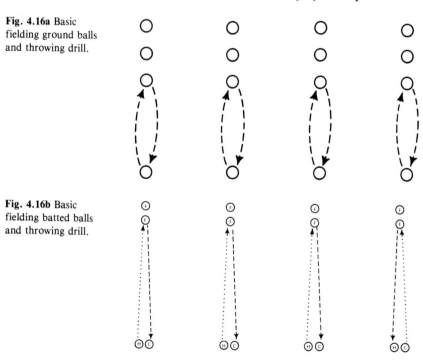

Fig. 4.16a Basic fielding ground balls and throwing drill.

Fig. 4.16b Basic fielding batted balls and throwing drill.

12. To practice running the group should be divided into pairs and lined up along the left or rightfield foul line. One partner runs forward sixty feet (the distance between bases) while the other one watches his running form. The runner runs back to foul line and is observed again. Partners discuss the good and bad points and possible corrections that need to be made. Reverse the roles.

13. To practice running use drill 12 but the runner runs in place while the partner observes.

14. To practice running to the left, right, or rear the player should assume the fielding position. A signal to move in a specified direction—right, left, or backward—is given. The player makes the correct pivot and begins to run.

15. To practice running the bases the players should line up at home. The teacher/coach stations himself by first base to observe the runners. The first player runs down the line, across the base and about ten yards down the foul line. The other players follow keeping about five yards between runners. Vary the drill by having the players continue to the next base(s).

Part II
The Offense

Chapter 5

Batting

Hitting a well-pitched softball effectively is a complex motor task. In the fast pitch game, making solid contact with a pitch of high velocity calls for a fearless attitude in combining quickness and strength with timing to react properly to the ball. Hitting a slow moving arched pitch, as in the slow pitch game, involves precision timing of the swing with strength to make contact at just the right moment in the curved path of the ball. Batters with great strength may consistently go for the "long ball" but it is the highly desirable line-drive, low trajectory type of hit that most performers should strive to master in either game. Generally, a short swing with good wrist action will produce sharply driven base hits while a long swing with straightened arms and full hip rotation yields the power needed for home runs.

A successful teacher/coach will develop techniques to help poor hitters make the adjustments necessary to ensure a degree of proficiency. Batting is a difficult skill to completely master because a complex interaction of factors must be consistently combined to provide a smooth and powerful swing. Proper instruction and practice in the fundamentals should help to improve the performance of individuals at every level.

Hitting Fundamentals

There are physiological, biomechanical, and psychological variables that combine to produce a good hitter. They should be considered by all students in softball.

The psychological factors are difficult to quantify. The individual's drive to practice hour after hour, his ability to concentrate on the task at hand, self-concept, and his desire to excel are not easily measured. The teacher/coach knows, however, that these qualities affect the ability to bat.

Mechanical attributes that produce good hitters have been determined by cinematographical analysis of six great baseball batters. They are:

1. The body's center of gravity followed a fairly level plane throughout the swing.
2. The head was adjusted from pitch to pitch to get the best and longest possible look at the flight of the ball.
3. The leading forearm tended to straighten at the beginning of the swing, thus resulting in greater bat speed.
4. The stride length was essentially the same for all pitches.
5. The upper body position, after contact, was in the same direction as the flight of the ball, thus the weight was transferred to the front foot.[1]

Knowledge of mechanical principles can also be important in batting. A bat with great weight (mass) swung with the same acceleration factor as a lighter bat will produce more force than the lighter bat. On the other hand, a light bat swung with increased acceleration could yield greater force than a heavier bat swung with less acceleration. It is the product of both acceleration and mass that produces force, therefore the proper bat to produce maximum force is one that can be optimally accelerated with respect to its weight according to the strength of the individual batter.

The performer must ultimately strive for control of the bat; great force at impact should not be the ultimate goal of all batters in all situations. In hitting for placement rather than power a different bat may be selected. Individual differences in size and strength of performers dictate the weights and lengths of bats to be selected.

In order to produce a line drive with high velocity and low trajectory, the batter must combine a level swing pattern with proper timing in the summing of forces of body segments. Primary contributing forces begin with the stride, move to the full rotation of the hips at impact, and conclude with the upper wrist rotating over the lower wrist just after impact and into the follow through. The ball should be contacted with full arm extension at close to 180° and struck through the center. The angle of projection must be less than 45° while closer to 30° would be more optimal to produce a low flight path.

The physiological or fitness components of strength, endurance, and flexibility are of great importance in performing the batting skill. The teacher/coach will need to help the player develop these attributes.

1. Guy G. Reiff, *What Research Tells the Coach About Baseball* (Washington D.C.: AAHPER, 1971), p. 2.

Key Points: Grip

1. Place the hands together, the right on top of the left, as the bat is gripped with the fingers, not the palms of the hands. (Fig. 5.1a)

    Gains proper control of the bat.

2. Align the middle knuckles of the top hand with the middle knuckles of the botton hand. (Fig. 5.1b) (Some batters choose to align the middle knuckles of the top hand with the area between the two rows of knuckles of the botton hand or to align the middle and large knuckles of both hands to form a straight and square line.) (Fig. 5.1c)

    Permits a greater range of motion in the wrist joint that can increase bat velocity.

3. Relax the grip initially but be firm on contact with the ball.

    Avoids unnecessary tension, recoil, and loss of power.

4. Turn the trademark of a wooden bat up.

    Presents edge grain of wood to prevent breaking.

Key Points: Stance (Fig. 5.2)

1. Plant the rear foot and keep the heel firmly in contact with the ground.

    Increases stability in the base of support.

Fig. 5.1a Gripping with the fingers to gain control of the bat.

Fig. 5.1b Gripping the bat by aligning the middle knuckles.

Fig. 5.1c Gripping the bat by aligning the middle knuckles with the large knuckles.

2. Spread the feet comfortably, about shoulder width apart.

   Establishes good balance and stability in the base of support.
3. Distribute the weight evenly between the feet; lean slightly forward on the balls of the feet.

   Maintains better balance and stability and helps in initially overcoming inertia.
4. Flex the hips and knees slightly.

   Increases stability and balance.
5. Keep the arms comfortably away from the body, the elbows six to nine inches away.

   Permits free movement and a full swing.
6. Hold the hands immobile, about shoulder high and over the rear foot.

   Allows for a full arm extension on the swing without dropping the hands or hitching the bat.
7. Hold the bat at a comfortable angle between vertical and horizontal.

   Permits a level and extended swing pattern for contact without unnecessary movement.

Fig. 5.2   Waiting for the pitch.

8. Keep the head still, focus the eyes on the ball, and tuck the chin close to the shoulder.

Eliminates unnecessary movements that contribute to an inconsistent swing pattern.

Key Points: Stride (Fig. 5.3)

1. Push off with the inside of the rear foot; keep the rear leg firm with the knee slightly flexed.

   Maintains stability and increases friction with the ground (particularly if wearing cleats).

2. Keep the weight on the rear foot.

   Permits proper timing in the summation of forces.

3. Stride forward toward the pitcher in a short (8 to 16 inches long) and low (3 to 4 inches high) glide rather than a step.

   Maintains balance and stability; helps overcome inertia smoothly; and allows for proper hip rotation that will increase the force of the bat at impact.

4. Keep the weight on the balls of the feet and pivot on the ball of the rear foot.

   Permits free movement in a forward direction.

Fig. 5.3 Striding.

Teaching/Learning Tips

1. Remind the batter to keep the rear foot firm and unmoving by placing dirt on top of his shoe.
2. Manually guide the batter in proper position by moving the arms and/or bat to the appropriate positions.
3. Remind the batter to keep the head firm and unmoving by placing a batting glove or similar light object on the head that must not fall off.
4. Check the consistency of the stride length by measuring the batter's stride on several good and poor hits. The distance between the footprints can be measured with a yardstick in a smoothed batter's box to indicate a good stride length for each individual. The negative aspects of overstriding will become obvious in the poorer hits.
5. Help establish a consistent stride once measured by marking the **optimal distance within the batter's box with a chalk line. Then** immediately check whether the batter is striding too long or too short and make corrections. (Fig. 5.4)

Fig. 5.4 Checking the stride length by placing a mark in the batter's box.

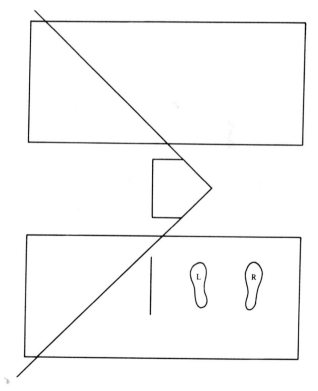

CONCEPT II: Proper swing and follow through contribute to effective hitting.

Key Points:

1. Start forward rotary action in the hips upon completion of the stride. (Fig. 5.5a)

    Yields maximum power on contact.

2. Rotate the shoulders and bat slightly backwards.

    Overcomes the inertia of the bat and increases the arc of the swing.

3. Keep the body weight back until just prior to contact.

    Produces highest acceleration and greatest force at contact.

4. Bring the hands forward but keep the head of the bat back. (Fig. 5.5b)

    Increases the speed of the bat resulting in increased power on contact.

Fig. 5.5a Bringing the bat around to get a level swing.

Fig. 5.5b Keeping the head of the bat back by leading with hands.

5. Keep the rear arm slightly flexed but bring the forward arm almost straight to full extension (a 180° angle, parallel to the ground is optimal) at contact. (Fig. 5.5c)

    Yields more power with a longer lever.

6. Whip the bat through the ball with a forceful wrist snap and full hip rotation.

    Increases the acceleration of the bat, increasing the force on impact.

7. Roll the top wrist over the bottom wrist just after impact. (Fig. 5.5d)

   Ensures that forces have been fully summated with a level and powerful swing.

8. Watch the ball carefully and keep the head firm and still until contact.

   Increases stability about the axis of rotation yielding greater force on the extended swing.

9. Hit through the center of the ball with the middle of the bat.

   Yields a solid and high type velocity of hit.

10. Bring the bat around in a full follow through. (Fig. 5.5e)

    Allows more force to be transferred to the ball.

Fig. 5.5c Contacting the ball with the nondominant arm extended and the dominant arm slightly flexed.

Fig. 5.5d Rolling the top wrist after the impact.

Fig. 5.5e Completing the follow through.

Teaching/Learning Drills

Many of the following may be practiced indoors without modification. Whiffle balls or nerf balls may replace the softballs, and a batting cage as well as old mats hung on the walls can increase the effectiveness of indoor practice.

1. To increase the ability to watch the ball, the batter may strike the ball from a stationary tee or from a string suspended overhead. Stop the swing just prior to impact and check for proper fundamentals in terms of the key points. Place a design, such as "X," on the ball where it should be contacted by the bat. The batter should watch the bat make contact with the mark.

2. To increase the ability to watch and focus on the ball, the batter

should stand at the plate and watch the ball from the time it leaves the pitcher's hand until it passes the plate. Try to actually see the stiches and the rotation of the ball. Place a colored design on the ball and have the batter name the color or design as the ball crosses the plate.

3. To practice watching the ball and hitting a ball traveling in an almost vertical plane, fungo. Toss the ball up high to allow time for two hands to be placed on the bat prior to the swing. Control the toss and swing to hit fly balls, ground balls, line drives, balls to the left side, and balls to the right side of the field.

4. To increase the ability to watch the ball until contact, lob the ball to the batter from six to eight feet away and have the batter hit the ball directly into a fence. The pitcher must be angled (at about 45°) out of the path of the ball; the fence should be ten to twelve feet from the batter. Challenge the batter to focus clearly on the seams of the ball. Vary the arch, speed, and location of the pitches. Pitcher and batter rotate after ten swings. (Safety precautions should be considered—and this may be appropriate for advanced players only.) (Fig. 5.6)

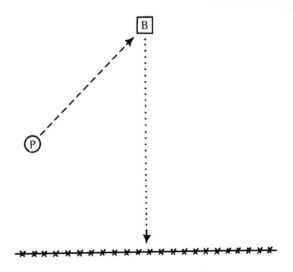

Fig. 5.6 Advanced batting practice drill.

5. To practice rolling the wrists properly, players should assume the proper grip and stance in any convenient area. Each player should stride and swing at imaginary pitches. Stress rolling the wrists when the arms are fully extended.

6. To practice keeping the head still during the swing, the batter should study his head movement by using his shadow. The

player should assume the proper grip and stance in any convenient area, with his shadow cast out front in full view. A marker should be placed on the shadow of the batter's head. After a full swing, if the head's shadow moves off the target, the head is moving too much.

7. To stress and practice the correct swing pattern, the concept of swinging down and through the ball must emphasized. This is not a chopping motion, but a level swing parallel to the ground. It can be practiced alone at various times throughout the practice session or as "homework." The key points must be stressed: hold the bat high and away, take a short glide step, turn the hips and shoulders together, extend the arms and hands fully over the plate, fix the eyes on the ball, keep the body weight over the rear foot, and bring the bat around in a full follow through.

8. To maximize swinging the bat a great number of times properly and hitting with placement, players should fungo balls against the screen or into the fence while waiting on deck for batting practice. A cloth target (two by four feet) may be placed on the fence, three feet above the ground. The batter stands back fifteen to twenty feet, tosses the ball up and hits at the target. This can be accomplished individually for varied lengths of time and should be combined with drill 7. The low target will force a level swing and produce line drives.

9. To assist in attaining a level swing, pull with the left hand instead of pushing with the right.

Bunting Fundamentals

Bunting should not be a neglected skill for any player on a fast pitch team, regardless of power or speed. There will be times when a baserunner must be advanced and the bunt becomes vital to team strategy. The bunt can be an important weapon for getting on base in addition to its obvious uses in sacrifice situations. Using the element of surprise in deceiving the defense to beat out a bunt for a base hit should not be overlooked in offensive strategy.

Temple has completed a comprehensive study to determine the most efficient velocity and direction for both sacrifice and base hit bunts.[2] Max-

2. Ina Temple, "Establishing Specific Objectives in Bunting," in *Softball Guide 1966-68*, (Washington D.C.: AAHPER, 1966), pp. 20-26.

imum running time to second base is yielded when a sacrifice bunt is hit with a velocity of ten feet per second and travels fifteen to twenty feet before it is fielded. This bunt should initially hit about four feet in front of the plate. (Fig. 5.7a) The desired velocity is greater on a base hit bunt, about sixteen feet per second, because the defense is much deeper. The ball should travel about thirty-five feet, initially hitting the ground about seven feet in front of home plate in order to yield the maximum running time to first base. (Fig. 5.7b) For either bunt, the most effective path of the ball is down the baselines, away from the pitcher and catcher. The baselines form a forty-five degree angle with the path of the pitch; therefore, the best bunt angle is between twenty-five degree and forty-five degree with the path of the pitch.

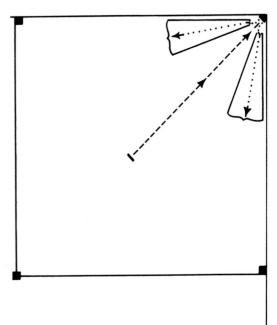

Fig. 5.7a Area in which to place a sacrifice bunt.

CONCEPT I: Proper body position contributes to effective bunting.

Key Points: The Square-around Stance (Fig. 5.8)

1. Master this basic stance before attempting others.

   Gives the batter sufficient time to set up and execute the bunt properly; however, the infielders also have sufficient time to adjust.

Fig. 5.7b Area in which to place a base hit bunt.

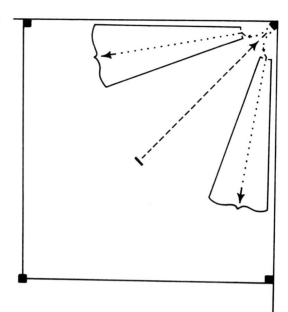

Fig. 5.8 Square-around stance.

2. Turn to face the pitcher just before the ball is released by the pitcher.

Sets the play early but still maintains a small degree of deception.

3. Take a quick step toward the outside of the batter's box with the front foot and bring the rear foot up even with it.

Permits the batter to squarely face the pitcher.

4. Place the feet with the toes pointing toward the pitcher, comfortably about shoulder width apart.

Establishes a stable base and efficient body position.

5. Flex the knees slightly.

Establishes a comfortable, stable position which allows control of the body.

Key Points: Pivot-in-the-Tracks Stance (Fig. 5.9a, b)

1. Master the advanced technique after mastering the square-around one.

Allows progression of mastery of a skill from the simple to the complex.

Fig. 5.9a Normal batting stance.

Fig. 5.9b Pivot-in-the-tracks stance.

2. Use the technique to deceive the defense.

   Allows the batter time for execution even though it is performed quickly.

3. Assume the normal batting stance as the ball is released.

   Sets the stage for deception.

4. Pivot on the heel of the front foot and the ball of the rear foot; do not lift the foot to step.

   Keeps the play hidden until the last possible moment.

5. Point the toes of the front foot directly at the pitcher while the rear foot turns just slightly toward first base.

   Places the body in position quickly.

6. Turn the hips and shoulders.

   Allows the batter to face the pitcher.

7. Crouch slightly and lean toward the plate.

   Permits the strike zone to be covered.

CONCEPT II: Proper bat position contributes to effective bunting.

Key Points: (Fig. 5.8)

1. Slide the top hand toward the trademark as the feet move.

   Permits good control of the bat for proper placement of the ball.

2. Grip the bat lightly with the sliding hand; keep the fingers underneath and the thumb on top and form a "V" with the thumb and forfinger.

   Gives control to the fingers rather than the palm, yielding increased ability to place the ball.

3. Hold the bat parallel to the ground, chest high, with the elbows slightly away from the body.

   Establishes the best position to hit down on the ball.

4. Focus the eyes on the ball from the pitcher's release to contact point.

   Yields a better chance to make good contact without distraction.

5. Keep the bat above the ball.

   Decreases the chances of popping up by forcing a hit down on the ball.

6. Adjust the entire body to the plane of the ball; flex the knees and arms as needed.

   Keeps the bat above the ball.
7. Contact the ball out in front of the plate.

   Decreases defense's time to see the play develop.
8. Give with the hands and arms on contact with the ball.

   Absorbs some of the force of the pitch and decreases the bunted ball's velocity.
9. "Catch" the ball with the bat as though it were a glove.

   Permits good bat control and absorbs the force from the pitch.

Strategy and Practice Fundamentals

Once the fundamentals of hitting and bunting have been introduced and practiced, emphasis should shift to the development of consistent individual playing patterns that will be successful for the performer and the team.

CONCEPT I: Varied forms of feedback will contribute to consistent hitting/bunting.

Key Points: Verbal Feedback

1. Know (teacher/coaches and players) enough about the various aspects to give immediate verbal feedback, both positive and negative.

   Reinforces the positive aspects while correcting the errors.
2. Give verbal feedback whenever possible on patterns as they develop in practice situations.

   Ensures practice of correct patterns.
3. Direct comments, not at isolated factors, but at repeated patterned movements.

   Focuses on the total picture rather than on a solitary element.
4. Develop confidence in the players to make personal corrections as well as offering reinforcement and/or corrections to their peers in a nonthreatening atmosphere.

   Yields increased educational benefits in skill development as well as in interpersonal relations.

Key Points: Visual Feedback

1. Enhance cognitive involvement by using a video tape recorder to play back the swing.

   Results in reinforcement of proper mechanics.

2. Construct the video tape recorder playback situation into a learning climate for all players through objective group analysis of each swing in comparison to the key points.

   Promotes positive interpersonal relationships as well as increasing the cognitive aspects.

3. Keep a notebook, noting the strengths and weaknesses of one's own team as well as opposing teams, for immediate and future use by teacher/coaches and players.

   Yields improved strategy planning.

Teaching/Learning Drills

1. To increase the cognitive involvement of all players and correct individual batting flaws, divide the group into pairs to observe and help each other. One partner will hit ten pitches in batting practice and be observed closely in terms of the key points. The observer will discuss flaws when poor patterns are noted in the majority of the swings. Partners then trade positions and repeat the sequence twice so that corrections may immediately be incorporated and practiced.

2. To practice using mental imagery before physically swinging the bat, the player should simply think through the key points. The batter may then imagine different pitches and actually swing the bat accordingly.

3. To practice perfecting the swing, previous drills may be repeated. (See pp. 47-49) Problems may be discussed between partners or among several players. Roles, the hitter and the observer, should be switched periodically.

CONCEPT II: Concentration and confidence are personal abilities that contribute to consistent hitting.

Key Points:

1. Know the dimensions of the strike zone and be able to distinguish balls from strikes in the practice situation.

   Increases confidence as the performer selects proper pitches to hit in the game situation.

2. Focus on the ball from the pitcher's hand until contact is made with the bat.

   Increases the chance of hitting successfully.

3. Select carefully the pitch to hit and hit with placement by going with the pitch. Inside pitches should generally go to the left field and outside pitches to right field.

   Increases the probability of hitting successfully.

4. Take each turn at bat in an aggressive though relaxed manner. (Moderate anxiety will generally increase motor performance while great stress causes performance to deteriorate.)

   Increases the probability of a smoothly coordinated attack on the ball.

5. Concentrate generally on meeting the ball well and not simply going for distance.

   Produces a higher batting average, more total times on base, and more runs scored in the long run.

Teaching/Learning Drills

1. To have players learn the strike zone, send a batter, pitcher, and catcher to the pitcher's warm-up area. The batter will assume a normal stance and watch the ball from release to the catcher's mitt. The batter does not swing, although he should imagine a good swing through mental practice, but calls each pitch a ball or strike and then checks with the catcher for accuracy. This should be used repeatedly for those who swing at bad pitches.

2. To teach players to hit the curve, each batter should receive about fifty percent curve balls in batting practice. The batter must watch the ball all the way, wait until the last moment before swinging and go with the pitch. The batter may choke the bat slightly and/or move to the front of the box to try to hit the pitch before it breaks.

3. To improve performance use a positive attitude. Batters should objectively analyze their performance in terms of the key points rather than emotionally berating themselves for poor hitting.

CONCEPT III: Batters must be able to consistently hit with placement to allow for the greatest advancement of runners.

Key Points:

1. To hit left select an inside pitch, open the stance by striding toward left field, and swing slightly late. (Fig. 5.10a)

Place hits the ball by going with the pitch.

2. To hit right select an outside pitch, close the stance by striding toward right field, and swing slightly late. (Fig. 5.10b)

   Place hits the ball by going with the pitch.

3. To hit straight-away select a pitch down the middle of the plate, square the stance by striding toward the pitcher, and swing with normal rhythm and timing. (Fig. 5.10c)

   Place hits the ball by going with the pitch.

Teaching/Learning Drills

1. To hit toward specific areas, set up various targets (cones on the field) and have the batters select proper pitches to hit toward prespecified targets.
2. To simulate game situations, place runners on specific bases and have the batters place hit to advance them.
3. To learn to go with the pitch, have the pitcher pitch to specified areas and have the batter hit to the prespecified targets.

CONCEPT IV: Varied situations dictate certain batting strategies.

Fig. 5.10a Open stance to hit to left field.

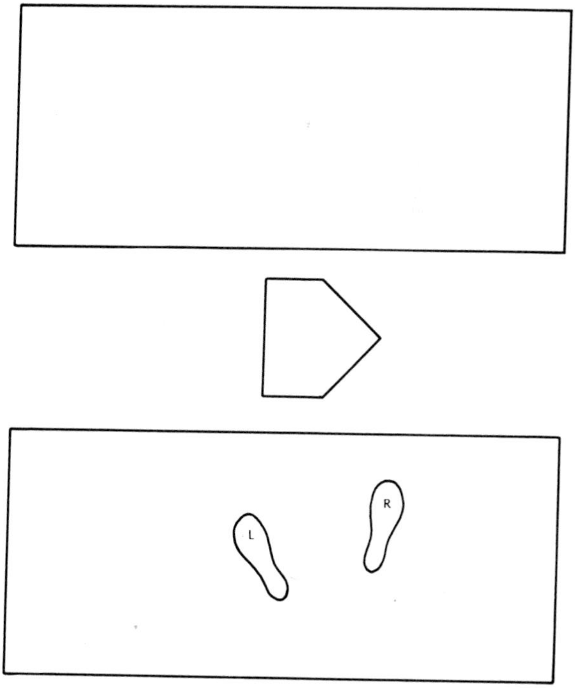

Fig. 5.10b Closed stance to hit to right field.

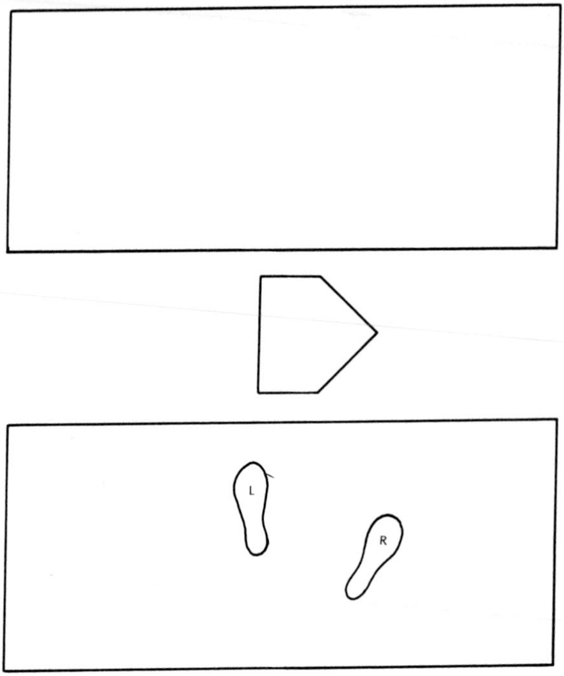

Fig. 5.10c Square stance to hit straight away.

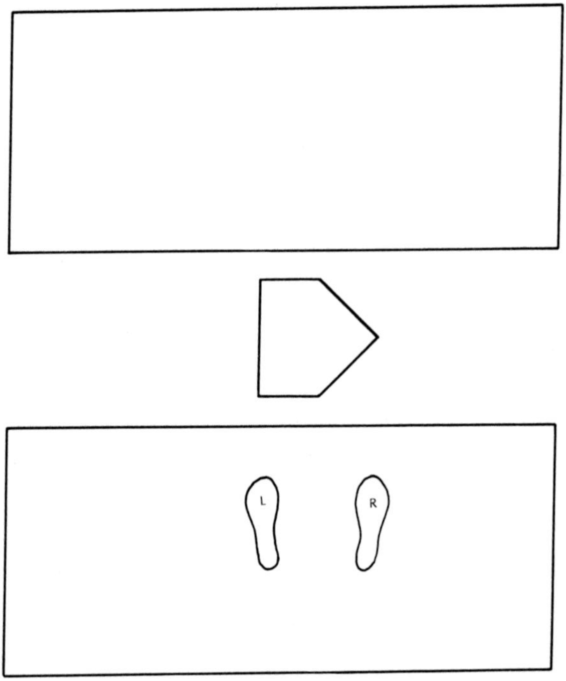

Key Points:

1. Hit the first good strike to your liking, preferably behind any runners.

   Gives the runners the best opportunity to score and reduces the possibilities of hitting into a double play.

2. Strive to stay ahead of the pitcher in the count.

   Decreases the chances of receiving marginal pitches and allows the batter to be offensive rather than defensive.

3. Wait for a strike before swinging when the preceding batter has just been put out after swinging at the first pitch.

   Prevents the pitcher from having a very quick and easy inning by possibly getting two outs with only two pitches.

4. Wait for a strike before swinging when the pitcher seems to be inconsistent.

   Forces the pitcher to work hard to throw strikes consistently.

5. Take the pitch (do not swing) on a 3-0 count unless directed to do otherwise by the coach.

   Gives an excellent chance for a walk.

6. Hit, or be ready to hit, on a 3-1 count.

   Increases probability that this will be a "fat" pitch, easy to hit well.

7. Avoid marginal and bad pitches with runners in scoring position when first base is occupied.

   Decreases the chance of being suckered by the pitcher who would like for the batter to go for a bad pitch rather than simply giving an intentional walk.

8. Hit the first good pitch against a pitcher with good control.

   Avoids getting behind in the count, forcing swings at marginal pitches.

9. Study the pitcher to find any pitching patterns.

   Allows the batter to become aggressive at the plate.

10. Hit to the right side of the field to give baserunners the best chance to advance.

    a. *Advances a runner from first to third on a base hit and decreases the possibility of a double play. Places the defense into the more difficult play to execute.*

    b. *Advances a runner from second on an infield out or a fly ball that is caught. Scores the runner on a base hit.*

11. Direct sacrifice flies to the outfielder with the weakest arm.

    Gives the runners a better opportunity to advance.

12. Attempt to meet the ball and go with the pitch on a two strike count.

    Allows better protection of the strike zone and decreases the chance of a strike out.

13. Keep the ball away from the pitcher and try to hit out of the infield completely with less than two outs and runners on first and second or bases loaded.

    Avoids the easy double play and ensures scoring at least one run.

14. Think and concentrate on executing the things you do best.

    Increases the chance of reaching base safely and advancing baserunners.

CONCEPT V: Varied situations call for certain bunting strategies.

Key Points:

1. Fake a bunt quickly and then slap a base hit past the defensive players as they adjust to the bunt.

   Forces defensive movement that can be used to the advantage of the batter.

2. Drag a bunt for a base hit after taking two full swings.

   Creates an element of surprise; the defense is not prepared for the play.

3. Bunt for a base hit more often in wet conditions.

   Increases the difficulty in fielding and throwing accurately.

Teaching/Learning Tips and Drills

1. To increase the use of the proper grip and hand position, place tape on the bat in the proper place for the batter to use in practice.

2. To practice absorbing force at contact, firmly attach an old glove to an old wooden bat with the fingers pointing up. Have the batter try to catch pitched balls in the glove by giving at impact. This may be practiced in pairs with a partner pitching and then rotating positions.

3. To practice the proper downward swing and contact with the lower portion of the bat, construct a half bat by slicing a wooden one through its length. Have the batter practice bunting with this bat, forcing a downward swing with the lower rounded portion of the bat. This may be practiced in pairs with a partner pitching and then rotating positions.

4. To practice bunting with the large end of the bat, cut off the handle of a wooden one. The batter is forced to use the large end for contact. This may also be practiced in small groups of two to four.

5. To practice bunting with the proper velocity and direction, set up markers as targets. Bats or chalk may be used to mark the optimal distances to yield proper velocity—fifteen to twenty feet on sacrifice bunts and about thirty-five feet on base hit bunts. Lines at four and seven feet from the plate can be drawn to mark the optimal touch down on the ground at the effective twenty-five degree to forty-five degree angle. Batters should work on this drill daily to master the speed and direction needed for both types of bunts.

6. To simulate game situations and practice the bunt, place runners at various bases. The batter will practice moving the baserunner—from first to second, second to third, third to home—and beating out the bunt for a single. (Fig. 5.11)

Fig. 5.11 Bunting, baserunning, and fielding drill.

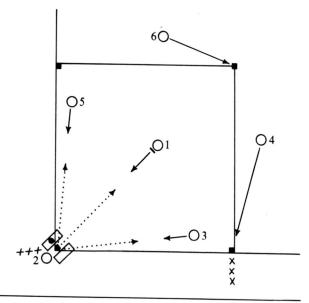

CONCEPT VI: A sacrifice bunt can be used to advance runners to scoring positions and eliminate the double play.

Key Points:

1. Bunt toward first base with a runner on first who must be advanced to second.

Decreases the chance of the first baseman making the play; throwing the runner out at second is most difficult from this position.

2. Bunt toward third base with the runners on first and second or just second.

   Decreases the chance of the third baseman making the play; throwing the runner out at third is most difficult from this position.

3. Bunt only at balls in the strike zone unless a suicide is called.

   Allows a better chance for a well-placed bunt.

4. Bunt the pitch wherever it is thrown when a suicide play is called.

   Protects the runner who has broken for the next base on the pitch.

5. Execute the suicide or the bunt and run play when the pitcher is behind in the count and is likely to make the next pitch a strike.

   Offers a better chance for proper execution.

6. Fake a bunt to check defensive adjustment.

   Gives the entire offense an opportunity to note defensive patterns with strengths and weaknesses apparent.

CONCEPT VII: The batter can surprise a defense playing deep or at normal depth by bunting for a base hit.

Key Points:

1. Conceal the bunt attempt until the last possible moment.

   Decreases the defensive time for reaction and proper execution.

2. Meet the ball on the move toward first base but remain in the batter's box until contact.

   Yields greater deception and decreases running time to first by overcoming inertia sooner.

3. Use the pivot rather than the square-around stance.

   Develops more quickly and is more deceptive.

4. Push or drag the ball toward the deeper player, either at first or third.

   Decreases the chance of the defense quickly fielding the ball.

5. Drop the rear foot back six inches on the pivot and slide the hand only halfway toward the trademark.

   Allows the play to develop quickly to maintain deception.

CONCEPT VIII: Good team play dictates making a full analysis of the opponent's strengths and weaknessss and strategically using these to an advantage.

Key Points: Infielders' Abilities

1. Pitcher is inconsistent—Wait for a strike.
2. Pitcher uses an unfamiliar pitching style—Carefully note the point of release rather than the entire motion.
3. Pitcher consistently throws the same type of pitch—Be aware of it and set up in the box accordingly.
4. Pitcher does not field well—Hit the ball back through the box.
5. Catcher does not field bunts well—Bunt the ball near home plate.
6. Catcher does not have a strong throwing arm—Be prepared to steal.
7. First or third baseman plays quite deep—Direct bunts in that direction for a base hit.
8. First or third baseman is awkward in bunt situations—Direct bunts to that player.
9. Second baseman and/or pitcher are not alert to cover in bunt situations—Direct more bunts toward first base.
10. First baseman is righthanded—Direct sharp hits to the available backhand hole.
11. Any player, particularly the third baseman, backs away from hard shots—Direct hard hit balls at that player.
12. Shortstop does not have a good range—Direct more balls between short and third to force a backhand stab and long throw to first.

Key Points: Outfielders' Abilities

1. Outfielder has a weak or erratic arm—Hit to that field and be prepared to take an extra base.
2. Outfielder has difficulty judging the ball in terms of wind, field conditions, and/or distance to the fence—Hit to that field and be prepared to take an extra base.
3. Fielders do not back each other up—Be prepared to take an extra base on all hits through to the outfield.
4. Outfielder has the arm to throw runners out at first base—Be aware of this and hustle aggressively on hits to that field.

CONCEPT IX: Batting slumps are temporary phenomena that seem to effect all batters at various times throughout the season and can be overcome.

Key Points or Causes:

1. Timing problems.
2. Losing eye contact with the pitch.
3. Swinging at bad pitches.
4. Playing while fatigued or injured; coming back from an injury too soon.
5. Overstriding.
6. Losing confidence and becoming overanxious.
7. Being distracted by unrelated emotional problems.

Teaching/Learning Tips and Drills

1. Participate in pepper drills without striding.
2. Concentrate on the flight of the ball and swing only at good strikes during batting practice.
3. Concentrate on meeting the ball in front of the plate with solid contact and hitting up through the middle of the diamond.
4. Hit for twenty minutes daily, beginning with less than a full swing to focus on solid contact and moving to the full swing after a day or two.
5. Change the weight and/or length of the bat; just change bats.
6. Bunt more often to force attention to the ball.
7. Rest properly and play only when recovered from injuries.
8. Choke up on the bat and hit to the opposite side of the field.
9. Alter the stance or position in relation to the plate.
10. Learn to relax at the plate and regain confidence.
11. Study video taped replays of the swing alone, with teammates, and/or with the teacher/coach.

Batting Order

There is no one set formula in devising a batting line-up. The batting order must be formed according to the strengths and weaknesses of the available players.

CONCEPT I: An optimal batting line-up will have the attack as strong as possible from beginning to end. The successful coach will place players in the line-up to produce the maximum number of runs scored in the game.

Key Points: First Batter

1. Have various ways to get on base.
2. Have a good eye to wait and draw walks; will not strike out.
3. Be small in stature to decrease the strike zone.
4. Be extremely quick with good baserunning ability.
5. Be a righthanded pull hitter to hit to the left side of the diamond and force the long throw across the infield.
6. Be a good bunter, able to bunt for a base hit.
7. Be a place hitter rather than a power hitter because there are fewer runs-batted-in (RBI).

Key Points: Second Batter

1. Be able to bunt consistently and accurately to advance the runner.
2. Have excellent bat control to advance the runner on the hit and run.
3. Have good speed and baserunning ability to score many runs.
4. Be able to hit behind the runner effectively.
5. Be lefthanded to hit naturally to the right side of the field to advance runners; a lefthanded batter also blocks the catcher's view of first and the throw to second on the steal.

Key Points: Third Batter

1. Be the most consistent hitter on the team.
2. Possess speed to prevent double plays and to take extra bases.

Key Points: Fourth Batter

1. Be the most powerful of the consistent batters on the team.
2. Be able to hit sacrifice flies and hit for extra bases to score many baserunners.

Key Points: Fifth Batter

1. Be the most powerful hitter.
2. Be able to score runners, similar to the fourth batter.

Key Points: Sixth Batter

1. Have lead-off batter qualities; possess speed, have the patience to wait for walks, and be a good bunter.
2. Have the power to score runners, as many will be on base.

Key Points: Seventh Batter

1. Have many second batter qualities, be lefthanded, able to execute the hit and run, and capable of bunting.
2. Hit to the right side to advance runners.

Key Points: Eighth Batter

1. Be the weakest batter in the regular line-up. (FP)
2. Be a powerful hitter to score runners; be the second clean-up batter. (SP)

Key Points: Ninth Batter

1. May be the pitcher to allow adequate rest in this weaker end of the line-up, rather than in the main run producing portion of the order. However, oftentimes the pitcher is one of the best hitters and will be placed higher in the order of batters. (FP)
2. Possess power to score runners; may have a low batting average. (SP)

Key Points: Tenth Batter

1. Have the lowest batting average on the team. (It is not necessary to give the pitcher a rest as it may be in fast pitch.)
2. Be the slowest runner. Speed ahead and behind this batter should avoid double play threats.

Key Points: General

1. Have pinch hitters available for crucial situations—sacrifice flies, place hitters to the right side, power hitters.
2. Place the most consistent hitters near the top of the order to ensure maximum times at bat and maximum runs scored.
3. Use substitutes in the late innings when the team is far ahead or far behind and occasionally in close games to give them necessary game experience.
4. Prepare a batting order that is a most strategic mixture of placement, power, and running speed.
5. Have pinch runners available for crucial situations calling for speed on the base paths.

Team Batting Drills

1. To practice hitting the ball up the middle, the batter must concentrate on hitting the ball squarely out in front of the plate. Cones may be set up as targets twenty feet on either side of second base. Two fielders cover this area and rotate with the batter and catcher. Each batter takes three swings and scores one point for hitting between the cones. The first batter to score five points wins. (Fig. 5.12)

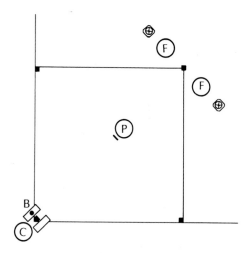

Fig. 5.12 Hitting through the middle drill.

2. To practice basic hitting and bunting fundamentals, players should be divided into three groups to bunt, hit live pitching, and hit off the batting tee. Players will rotate stations after twenty minutes. The bunting may be done behind the backstop, batting with the tee on the right field line, and hitting live pitching on the playing field. (Fig. 5.13)

3. To practice hitting behind the runner on the hit and run play, an offensive team will play against a defensive team. As soon as the pitcher releases the ball the runner on first breaks for second. The second baseman will move to cover second on the steal and the batter should hit through the vacated hole. Each member of the offensive team gets one swing while members of the defensive team try to prevent the runner from taking third base. Each player will get two chances to advance the runner before the two teams switch roles. The team which successfully advances the most runners is the winner.

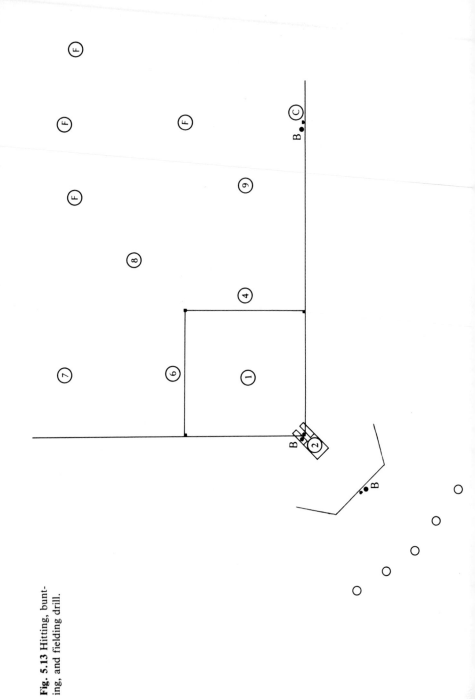

Fig. 5.13 Hitting, bunting, and fielding drill.

4. To give batters practice hitting under pressure, each batter takes a 3-2 count with runners on second and third. Both runners break for home when they are legally able and the batter must swing at the pitch. Offense trades off running the bases and hitting; each hitter gets two chances before the two teams switch roles. After two complete sequences, the total number of runs scored determines the winner.

5. To simulate game conditions, players should be divided into three teams of five. Players should be distributed among the teams according to positions played to adequately cover on defense and practice in normal situations. One team of five players will bat with three outs per inning for three consecutive innings against the other two teams of five and then rotate to the defense. Runners are removed from the bases at the end of each inning. Players coach the bases and the team of five scoring the most runs wins. One-pitch softball may be played as an alternate, in which the batter gets only one pitch to hit into fair territory. The pitcher is on the offensive team and makes no defensive plays. Each member of the offense, including the pitcher, will bat before rotating to defense rather than on three outs. Players must hustle in and out because the batter may hit as soon as the pitcher and batter are ready.

6. To force the batter to concentrate on what to look for on various counts, plan an intra-squad game with each batter assuming the same count, example, 3-0, 1-2. Vary the count from day to day in order to have practice situations under flexible conditions. This will also help the pitchers concentrate on the pitch needed in particular situations.

Chapter 6

Baserunning

Aggressive baserunning is an asset to both slow pitch and fast pitch teams. Speed is certainly desirable in baserunners but alertness combined with knowledge of the situation and proper sliding mechanics can produce fine baserunning from slower players. Baserunning should begin in the dugout, not simply after the ball has been hit. All players should study the pitcher, fielders' range and throwing accuracy, defensive placement, field and wind conditions—anything that could have some effect on baserunning, once that opportunity actually comes. Most successful runners agree that concentration and effective practice can make players of average ability into real threats on the base paths. The good baserunner will force breaks by thinking ahead, gambling on the extra base, and reacting immediately to defensive hesitations or errors. This style of play will win games as well as add extra excitement to the game.

Baserunning Fundamentals

The batter becomes a baserunner as soon as the ball is hit into fair territory. He should not wait at the plate until the umpire calls the ball fair or foul, but should begin to run toward first as soon as the ball is hit. The batter/baserunner has plenty of time to return to the plate if the cry is "foul ball." There are times when a ball is obviously going into foul territory and there is no need to run on those. However, if the ball goes forward, the batter should run!

CONCEPT I: The batter should follow certain guidelines to become an effective runner and maximize scoring opportunites.

Key Points: Running to First Base

1. Take the first step toward first base with the rear foot.

   Gives greater push-off and momentum.

2. Run in a straight line to the base and with full speed and effort on all hit balls.

   Decreases the time and distance needed; the most routine balls may be misplayed.

3. Run smoothly across the base; do not jump or leap for the base; and step on the front outside part of the base. (Fig. 6.1)

   Maintains speed in reaching the base and avoids possible collisions.

Fig. 6.1 Running across first to a target past the base.

4. Aim for a target beyond the base, about five yards past, and slow down only after crossing the target.

   Maintains speed in reaching the base.
5. Slide into first only to avoid a tag and/or collision when the first baseman has been pulled into the baseline.

   Avoids reducing momentum unnecessarily.
6. Assume responsibility for knowing when the throw gets by the first baseman.

   Permits the extra base to be taken without a delay.
7. Take an aggressive turn at first.

   Pressures the defense to field the ball quickly.
8. Run on the inside edge of the restraining line whenever the ball is fielded in the home plate area.

   Reduces the size of the thrower's target.

Fig. 6.2a, b Placing the body into position to watch the ball when returning to the base.

9. Turn to face the outfielder making the play on the ball after rounding first and coming back to the base—turn the right shoulder toward the infield to pivot back on a ball hit to the right side and turn the left shoulder toward the infield to come back on a ball hit to the left side. (Fig. 6.2a, b)

Allows the ball to be watched all the way.

Key Points: Running for Extra Bases (Fig. 6.3a, b, c)

1. Swing into foul territory about eight to ten feet before reaching first, tag the inside of the base in full stride and pivot toward second.

   Yields the most efficient path with the greatest momentum.
2. Hit the base with the inside, left foot and cross-over with the

Fig. 6.3a Rounding first base and going to second. Pick up the first base coach before reaching first and the third base coach before reaching second.

Fig. 6.3b Rounding first and second bases and going to third. Pick up the first and third base coaches.

Fig. 6.3c Going home.

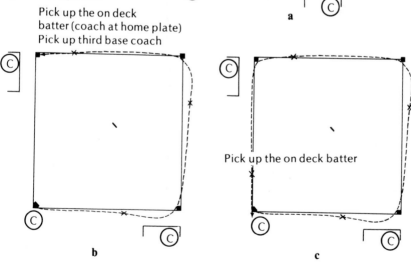

Pick up third base coach

Pick up first base coach

a

Pick up the on deck batter (coach at home plate)
Pick up third base coach

Pick up the on deck batter

b

c

outside foot and lean toward second. Do not break stride to accomplish this. (Fig. 6.4)

Permits the greatest push-off while maintaining momemtum.

3. Take advantage of the outfielders fielding the ball on the nonthrowing side.

Increases throwing time from the outfield.

4. Straighten the path and run in a flattened arc from third to home.

Runs the most direct route.

5. Keep the head up to view the entire situation—the coaches, the ball, and the defensive players.

Decreases put-out possibilities while running aggressively.

Fig. 6.4 Hitting the base with the inside foot when preparing to take the next base.

Teaching/Learning Tips and Drills

1. To practice varied baserunning situations, batters should run on every other hit during batting practice.

2. To practice running with proper form from home to first, all players should run this route several times. This drill can be extended to run to second, to third, and all the way around the bases.

3. To add incentive to better personal times in subsequent practices, time each player as drill 2 is practiced.

CONCEPT II: Each baserunner should follow certain guidelines to become an effective runner and maximize scoring opportunities.

Key Points: Running the Bases

1. Run aggressively early in the game.

   Tests the defense and could cause early errors.
2. Have faith in the base coaches; hesitation will bring disaster.

   Gives those with the better vantage point the decision making responsibility.
3. Pick up the third base coach ten to twelve feet before reaching second base and pick up the on-deck batter for signals as you come into home.

   Gives good position for proper decisions and allows time for the runner to react to the signal.
4. Check the entire defensive situation each time you are on base.

   Decreases the chance of making a mistake.
5. Gamble on the bases when your team is ahead but run more cautiously when your team is behind in the late innings.

   Decreases the chance of losing a needed scoring opportunity.
6. Tag up on all bases on any fly ball that will be foul.

   Gives a good chance to make the next base if the defense is not alert.
7. Go hard all the way into second and slide when a play is made there.

   Helps break up double play chances; routine balls may be misplayed.
8. Start high and shift the weight low just before the catch is made on tag up plays.

   Initiates the overcoming of inertia to gain momentum.
9. Run into any defensive player who is obstructing the baseline on rundowns.

   Gives the runner the next base as the defensive player is in an illegal position.

Key Points: Specific Situations

1. Runner on first, less than two outs—If the third baseman fields the bunted ball, the runner should be alert to take third if the catcher or pitcher is not covering.
2. Runner on second, less than two outs—If the third baseman or shortstop goes deep into the hole to make the long throw to first, an alert runner can advance, once the fielder has released

the ball. The runner could also try to distract the fielder from throwing the runner out at first by drawing attention to himself.

3. Runner on third, less than two outs—A runner should not anticipate leaving the base on a fly ball to the outfield; the runner must stay on the base until the ball touches the fielder's glove or it is very obvious that the ball will not be caught. A base hit will easily score the runner; a clean tag up can be made on a sacrifice fly; and a great catch (which comes most unexpectedly) will not find the runner madly scrambling back to third to tag up and thus, reduce the chance of scoring that run.

4. Tag up situation, less than two outs—The base coach should give the auditory signal "go!" along with the visual arm signal when the fly ball is approximately one foot from the outfielder's glove. The small amount of time between the signal and the runner's movement off the base is accounted for by the runner's reaction time. As the ball hits the glove, the runner will be assured of the most efficient tag. A juggled catch will not penalize the runner because he may leave as soon as the ball is initially touched, the runner need not and should not wait for the fielder to gain full possession of the ball to leave.

5. Runner on third base—The runner should stand with one foot on the base and the other foot in foul territory and move completely into foul territory as soon as legally possible to avoid the chance of being hit by a struck ball in fair territory and thus be called out.

6. Runners on first and/or second base, less than two outs—Runners should lead off part way on short flies to the outfield and about half way on sinking flies or possible shoe-string catches in order to draw a rushed throw from the outfielder as the runner hustles back on the caught ball. The forward distance should never be too far to retreat safely if the ball is caught. This daring action gives good position to avoid the force out at the next base should the ball not be caught on the fly but well fielded and thrown quickly to that base. Because the fielder is usually less prepared to make an accurate throw behind the runner, the play for the fielder's choice is the more routine play and must be avoided by the baserunner.

7. Runners on first and/or second base, less than two outs—Runners should remain on the base on long fly balls that will be caught until the catch and then move quickly to take the next base or to draw a rushed throw and then take the next base on the misplay.

8. Runners on first and third, less than two outs—On a short fly to

the outfield, the runner on first should tag up and advance hoping to draw the throw to second base so that the runner on third may score.

9. Runners on first and third—On a short passed ball or wild pitch, the runner on first should advance to second and attempt to draw the long throw, which may allow the runner on third to score.

10. Runner on first or on second, less than two outs—On a base hit, when the runner advances to third, it is imperative that the batter/baserunner take second in order to avoid an easy force or double play situation on the next batter. To facilitate this move, the runner at third should round the base and draw attention away from the runner moving to second. Under no conditions should the lead runner go so far as to be caught in a rundown or be thrown out; this is not a sacrificial situation. However, the batter/baserunner may strategically sacrifice himself going into second by drawing the throw and enabling the run to score. The game situation would dictate whether trading an out for a run would be desirable.

11. Lead runner caught in a rundown, less than two outs—The runner should attempt to advance to the next base only and not return because the trailing runner will advance to that base during the rundown. This aggressive style of running, going for advancement at both bases, should be considered more by conservative coaches. With two outs, the lead runner should be given a base to retreat to safely.

12. Runner on first, less than two outs—When a ground ball is hit to the second baseman in front of the runner, the runner should stop and force a play rather than just running into the tag. If the grounder is hit behind the runner, he should take a path to distract the throw from the fielder to the shortstop covering second.

Teaching/Learning Drills

1. To practice taking extra bases, runners should begin at first base. The coach will fungo singles to center and right fields and the runner will go all the way to third, without slowing down. A hook slide to avoid the tag may be practiced.

2. To practice taking an extra base, all infielders, base coaches, and runners will participate. Runners begin at varied bases. The coach fungoes to any infielder who fields the ball and then tosses it away from himself, simulating an error. The runner breaks for the next base on the error as the infielder goes after

the ball and attempts to make the play. Fielders may occasionally make a clean play to keep the runners from cheating and possibly create an opportunity to practice the rundown situation.

3. To practice getting the batter to second base, begin play with a runner on the base. The coach will fungo a single to any part of the field and the runner on second will move to third and round the base to allow the runner starting from home to advance to second.

4. To practice tagging up properly on long fly balls, all coaches and all players will take their positions. Runners will be assigned to various bases and the coach will fungo long fly balls and line drives throughout the outfield. Runners will tag up properly and move to the next base. Fielders and runners should be rotated throughout this drill to ensure all players the chance of tagging at various bases on varied fly balls.

5. To practice moving properly from varied bases on long and short fly balls, drill 4 can be repeated with softer line drives and flies.

6. To practice all baserunning techniques, drills 4 and 5 can be combined with all the infielders, outfielders, base coaches, and runners participating. Varied types of hits will be scattered by the coach as the runners concentrate on the fundamentals of baserunning.

7. To end a practice in a challenging manner and practice tagging up on sacrifice flies, spread all the outfielders in their fields. All other players line up at third base except the catcher who assumes his normal position. The coach fungoes fly balls and the runners tag up and try to score. Runners thrown out return to the base to run again while the outfielder making the play comes off the field. Runners safe at home come off the field while that outfielder making the throw stays out for another play.

Sliding Fundamentals

Sliding is a most important component in aggressive baserunning. Any slide should be considered as a controlled fall rather than a leap or jump into the base because the momentum built from the run will carry the runner into the base properly. The major purpose of sliding, that is to stop quickly at a base, should be accomplished with a basic bent leg slide performed on the preferred side of the body. Advanced players should learn to slide on both sides of the body in order to facilitate the other purposes for sliding—to evade tags and possible collisions. Hook slides best accomplish these purposes. Once the decision has been made to slide, the player should relax and go through with it in good form and with proper mechanics, in order to avoid injury.

CONCEPT I: The bent leg slide should basically be used to stop quickly at a base.

Key Points: Bent Leg Slide (Fig. 6.5a, b, c)

1. Begin about eight to ten feet from the base.

   Yields proper momentum.

2. Take off on the natural or more comfortable leg.

   Gives more efficiency and possibly more confidence.

3. Bend the take-off leg at the knee; place it under the extended leg and keep it parallel to the ground.

   Yields proper position to avoid injury.

4. Place the foot of the bent leg sideways.

   Avoids the problem of the spikes catching in the ground.

5. Stretch the leg that will touch the base forward with the knee only slightly flexed.

   Permits the quickest touch while keeping the spikes off the ground.

6. Contact the front part of the base with the heel of the extended leg.

   Helps to absorb force and reduce momentum while remaining in contact with the base.

7. Throw the upper body back and keep the arms and hands up off the ground.

   Helps to avoid injury.

8. Use the abdominal muscles to keep the upper back from touching the ground.

   Gives proper position for popping to the feet and possible advancement.

9. Arch the neck to keep the eyes on the tag and the base.

   Helps to avoid a tag and/or a collision.

10. Absorb the force of the slide in the buttocks.

    Avoids injury to more fragile body parts—fingers, ankles or knees.

11. Shift the weight forward and upward at contact with the base.
   Allows for the pop-up to the feet in readiness to take the next base.

Fig. 6.5a Beginning the bent leg slide. The baseman is waiting to receive a throw from the leftfielder.

Fig. 6.5b Approaching the base.

Fig. 6.5c Stretching the leg to touch the base as quickly as possible.

CONCEPT II: The hook slide should be used to evade tags and avoid collisions.

Key Points: Hook Slide (Fig. 6.6a, b, c, d)
   1. Begin six to eight feet from the base.
      Produces proper momentum; more speed is needed than in the bent leg slide.

2. Hook to the side opposite the throw.

   Gives advantage in avoiding the tag.

3. Bend the hooking leg at the knee after take-off.

   Allows for proper positioning.

4. Place the foot of the hooking leg sideways with the instep facing the base.

   Avoids catching the cleats in the ground.

5. Extend the touching leg with the foot pointing slightly upward.

   Offers the quickest touch and keeps the cleats off the ground.

6. Throw the body off to the side of the base; catch the corner of the base with the toe only.

   Offers the defense a small area to tag.

7. Bend the touching leg only upon contact with the base.

   Gives the quickest touch and helps absorb force.

8. Keep the arms and hands off the ground.

   Avoids injury.

9. Keep the eyes focused on the fielder's hands and the tag.

   Increases the chance of avoiding the tag.

Fig. 6.6a Beginning the hook slide.

Fig. 6.6b Approaching the base.

Fig. 6.6c Throwing the body off to the side of the base.

Fig. 6.6d Bending the touching leg upon contact with the base. The hands should be held up rather than placed on the ground.

Key Points: Hook and Roll

1. Begin with the regular hook slide about six feet from the base. (Fig. 6.7a)

   Gains necessary momentum; more is needed for this slide.

2. Pull the hooking leg away from the tag by straightening it. (Fig. 6.7b)

   Allows the body to slide past the base, avoiding an imminent tag.

3. Slide past the base with both legs straight and roll over to the chest.

   Gives the momentum to slide past the tag.

4. Reach bag and grab the back corner of the base. (Fig. 6.7c)

   Establishes the best position to surprise the defense and avoid the tag completely.

Fig. 6.7a Beginning the regular hook slide.

Fig. 6.7b Straightening the hooking leg while sliding past the base.

Fig. 6.7c Reaching back to touch the base after rolling into a prone position.

Teaching/Learning Drills

1. To receive initial instruction, players should be in a circular formation in soft grass with the shoes off, long pants on, and with unattached bases as targets. The coach gives group and individual instruction, reinforcement, and correction from the center position. A sliding pit, which can easily be constructed with sand or sawdust, can be used for further individualized instruction.

2. To practice hook sliding on both sides of the body and away from the tag, small groups should be formed at different bases. As the ball is tossed to one side of the base, the slide is executed to the other side (ball tossed right, slide left; ball tossed left, slide right).

3. To practice the pop-up motion to the feet, peers can assist the performer by pulling on the slider's arms just after contact with

the base. This form of manual guidance allows the learner to experience the proper kinesthetic feeling for the movement.

4. To practice keeping the arms up and the body down in executing all slides, a bat can be held above the sliding area. The slider's body must pass beneath the bat while the arms and hands reach up to touch. (Fig. 6.8)

Fig. 6.8 Basic sliding drill stressing keeping the head, shoulders, and arms up.

5. To practice the hook slide, divide the group into smaller groups and move to the outfield grass. Players should be in long pants and stocking feet to reduce the chance of injury. Place a base sixty feet in front of each line and a second base sixty feet further. On "go" the first player in each line sprints to and hooks to the left of the first base, jumps up and runs to the next base for a hook slide to the right. This player then races back to tag the next player in his line. The sequence is repeated until everyone has had at least two trials. (Fig. 6.9)

6. To practice hook sliding or hooking and rolling away from the

Fig. 6.9 Hook sliding drill.

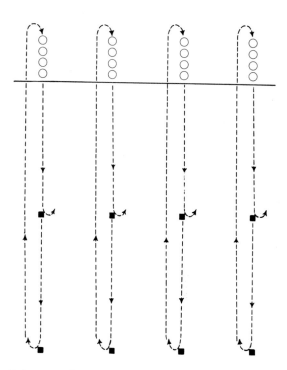

tag, have the pitcher, catcher, second baseman, and shortstop assume their positions. The runners will line up behind first base and break for second on the pitch. The catcher will throw to the base with the two infielders alternating the coverage. The runner must concentrate on the eyes and hands of the player making the tag in order to hook or hook and roll away from the tag.

7. To practice the bent leg slide with the pop-up to the feet, all players will line up at the plate. Each player in turn will swing at an imaginary pitch and run all the bases. The runner will use the bent leg slide and pop-up at second and third and then hook slide into home. The coach may time each runner as an incentive to improve baserunning and sliding techniques.

CONCEPT III: Base the selection of the best slide for a particular situation on the strategy needed.

Key Points:

1. Use head first slides sparingly even though they are the most mechanically efficient ones. (Fig. 6.10)

   Increases the danger of injury to the hands, arms, and heads as

Fig. 6.10 Sliding head first.

these body parts are exposed to the cleats of the defensive player.

2. Use the bent leg slide in most force situations as it is the safest and the quickest in stopping momentum.

   Permits the quickest touch and best position for regaining the feet to advance further when possible.

3. Use the hook slide to avoid tags.

   Allows for greater maneuverability; it is a slower maneuver than the bent leg slide.

4. Use the hook and roll only in emergency situations.

   Avoids threatened tags with a last ditch deceptive movement.

Stealing Fundamentals

Teams that use the steal effectively are able to get runners into scoring position without using the sacrifice and giving up an out. In addition this asset, the steal or the threat of a steal, can rattle the defense and cause mistakes. The pitcher may be distracted from full concentration on the batter. The second baseman and shortstop must move to cover for the throw and leave large holes for the batter to attack. Each baserunner should be prepared to steal—either on sheer personal speed or by taking full advantage of defensive distractions or hesitations.

CONCEPT I: Use a rockaway start to move from the base quickly on each pitch.

Key Points: (Fig. 6.11)

1. Place the heel of either foot in contact with the part of the base closest to the next base and place the toes in contact with the ground, pointing toward the next base.

   Gives a push-off point to quickly gain momentum.

2. Place the other foot one step behind the base and pointing directly at the next base while assuming a slightly crouched position.

   Yields a quick start without leaving the base too soon.

3. Time the pitcher's motion so that the first step on the rear foot will be completed and the front foot will leave the base on the pitcher's release.

   Gives the quickest legal start with the greatest momentum.

4. Lead off the base exactly the same way on each pitch and appear to be taking the next base regardless of your specific intention on that pitch.

   Adds pressure to the defense by increasing the deceptive tactics.

Fig. 6.11 Preparing to leave a base quickly by using the rockaway start.

CONCEPT II: The baserunner must be constantly alert to pressure the defense and take advantage of forced hesitations, mental lapses, or outright errors in order to steal more effectively.

Key Points:

1. Lead off each time far enough to draw a throw but not so far as to be picked off by the catcher.

   Results in defensive misplays.

2. Be prepared to dive back quickly to the base if necessary.

   Gives the quickest return, though somewhat dangerous.

3. Take the next base without hesitation on a poor throw or fumbled catch on a pick-off play.

   Gives an advantage that must not be lost.

4. Watch the ball carefully and break for the next base on a poor or lob throw to the pitcher, particularly when the defense is deep.

   Catches the defense off guard; gives time to advance.

CONCEPT III: There are certain general strategies that contribute to an effective steal.

Key Points:

1. Do not steal when your team is several runs behind.

   Reduces the chance of the big inning; the risk of being thrown out for the advancement of one base is too great.

2. Do not steal when your team has a big lead late in the game.

   Avoids taking advantage of a lesser skilled team by running up the score; avoids the unnecessary risk of injury.

3. Steal second with a lefthanded batter up.

   Gives the catcher a more difficult throw.

4. Steal on a curve ball or change of pace more often than on a fast ball.

   Increases the running time on a slower pitch.

5. Do not steal with a weak hitter up and two out.

   Leaves the weak hitter to lead off the next inning should you be out.

6. Execute a double steal by having the trailing runner commit himself first.

   Encourages the catcher to throw to stop the trailing runner; the lead runner may then advance.

Teaching/Learning Drills

1. To practice the rockaway start, group instruction may be given in a circular formation and partners may be used to check for proper mechanics. The coach in the center will simulate the pitching motion and give the auditory signal "go" at the release point, all players will start and take several steps before returning. Individuals should further practice this start when running the bases during batting practice.

2. To practice the squeeze play, line up runners at third base. The runner will break on the pitcher's release with the rockaway start and the batter must bunt the ball. All players should rotate between playing defense, practicing the run, and taking three bunts.

3. To practice the double steal, line runners up at first and third with the infield in position. The runner on first may also begin a steal and try to become trapped in a rundown to allow the run to score. Remember, the runner at third breaks for the plate only when the throw has gone to second or when the defense becomes involved in the rundown. This lead runner should not be faked and trapped off third base.

Coaching the Bases

Those who take the important role of coaching the bases should be intelligent, able to make quick decisions, possess good common sense, know the rules, know the abilities of all players on the field (both offense and defense), be analytical and be able to remain calm in tense situations. Such people are rare indeed. All players should be afforded the opportunity to develop these capabilities; the educational potential is tremendous. Players given appropriate instruction, sufficient practice, and game experience in coaching the bases will develop the knowledge, competence, and confidence needed to perform well. In this intense learning situation, players can develop responsibility, decision-making ability, and total involvement with the game. This role may be filled by a manager, a coach, or a player; the choice lies in the philosophy of the person in charge of the group.

Many runs can be scored by teams who use aggressive and competent baserunning as part of the offensive attack. The primary responsibility of the base coaches is to assist the runner in advancing around the bases and scoring by whatever legitimate means are possible. Players must have faith in their coaches and comply with their decisions. Baserunning pressure should be applied at every opportunity to force defensive mistakes. This climate is produced only with the deliberate and well practiced efforts from both the runners and the coaches. Coaches must never become so caught up in the excitement of the game that runners, particularly trailing runners, are forgotten.

CONCEPT I: Base coaches must perform certain general duties.

Key Points:

1. Remind the runner of the following:
   a. the number of outs, the score, the count on the batter.
   b. the importance of that runner's particular run, whether it is the winning, tying, or needed to catch up run; these would be played more cautiously.
   c. the possible plays coming up and the runner's responsibility; example, to break up a double play.
   d. to be alert for caught line drives.
   e. to be alert for passed balls or wild pitches.
   f. to keep an eye on the catcher when leading off the base.
   g. when to leave on a steal.
   h. to go half way on shallow flies and to tag on long flies.

   Stays aware of all situations and sets up scoring opportunities.

2. Decide on risks and strategy as the game demands. When the team is behind, fewer chances should be taken. When the team is ahead or early in the game, aggressive baserunning is the rule.

   Uses strategies to fit the situation.

3. Keep up a steady chatter of encouragement and instructions to each runner.

   Holds the runner's attention.

4. Watch the ball and the defensive players carefully.

   Alerts the runners to fakes and avoids careless errors.

5. Study the opposition carefully player by player before and during the game in terms of speed, fielding, and throwing ability.

   Helps make informed decisions for the baserunner.

6. Stay within the designated coaching box and do not physically assist runners to come to or leave the base.

   Avoids interfering with the play.

CONCEPT II: Base coaches must perform certain specific duties.

Key Points: First Base

1. Relay any offensive signals to the runner, example, bunt, hit, and run.

   Prepares the runner in advance for the set play.

2. Encourage the batter before each pitch to get on base and further encourage the batter to beat out any hit ball, with no runners on.

   Gives support to the batter.

3. Pick up the batter as soon as the ball is struck, tell and signal whether to go for second as soon as you have located the ball.

   Permits the batter to concentrate on running.

4. Instruct the runner to take the turn and watch the ball on a base hit out of the infield. When possible, tell the runner to take second without hesitation; example, when the ball is fumbled in the outfield or when an errant throw is made back to the infield.

   Takes advantage of defensive miscues.

Key Points: Third Base

1. Give or relay offensive signals to the batter and baserunner.

   Alerts the players to the offensive team's plans.

2. Pick up the runner going into second or third about fifteen feet before the base and signal whether to continue, stop, or round the base and look.

   Gives the runner time to adjust.

3. Remind the runner on third of the following:
   a. to take the legal lead into foul territory, avoiding the out if struck by a line shot.
   b. to stay alert for passed balls, wild pitches, or a possible steal.
   c. to remain on the base and tag on all flies to the outfield.
   d. to be aware of the number of outs and the position of the infielders for a possible scoring attempt on an infield put-out or to draw defensive attention away from the runner

going to first; again, this lead runner must not be trapped or caught in a rundown.

Prevents mistakes and increases the chances of scoring.

CONCEPT III: Certain signals should be given to batters and baserunners. (The particular signals should be simple and may be created by each coach and team.)

Key Points: Specific Situations

1. The take—the batter must not swing at the next pitch but look for a walk.

   Gets the batter on base.
2. The hit sign—a definite sign to allow the batter to swing in certain situations, example, the 3-0 count.

   Alerts the batter to possible situations.
3. Hit and run—the batter must hit the ball on the ground to protect the runner who has broken for the next base on the pitcher's release.

   Decreases the chances of a play being made on the lead runner.
4. Run and hit—the runner will go on the pitch and the batter will hit the ball if it is a strike; if not, the runner steals on his own. Generally given on a 3-1 or 2-0 count when the next pitch should be a strike.

   Takes advantage of the chance that the pitch will be a choice one to hit.
5. Bunt and run—the batter must bunt whether the pitch is a strike or not.

   Protects the runner who has broken for the next base on the pitcher's release.
6. Sacrifice—the batter bunts only a pitch that is a strike, the runner does not break for the next base until the ball is bunted on the ground.

   Avoids hitting a bad pitch when attempting to advance the runner.
7. Safety squeeze bunt—the batter bunts only a pitch that is a strike, the runner from third does not break for home until the ball is bunted on the ground.

   Avoids hitting a bad pitch when attempting to get the runner home.

Key Points: Signals

1. Rotate one arm in a vigorous circle to have a runner continue to the next base. Call out the instruction "go" at the same time. Be sure not to get too close to the runner in your enthusiasm. (Fig. 6.12a)

   Gives distinct signals that can be seen and heard.

2. Throw one arm up above the head and the other at a right angle in the direction of the next base if the runner has time to take the base and make a short turn. Call out the instruction "turn" at the same time. (Fig. 6.12b)

   Gives distinct signals that can be seen and heard.

3. Hold both arms straight up over the head if the runner has time to take the base but must remain on it with no turn. Call out the instruction "stay here" at the same time. (Fig. 6.12c)

   Gives distinct signals that can be seen and heard.

4. Point the palms of both hands downward with the arms extended if the runner must slide. Call the instruction "hit it" at the same time. A sweeping motion of holding the arms to one side of the base should indicate on which side the player should slide in order to avoid the tag. (Fig. 6.12d)

   Gives distinct signals that can be seen and heard.

Fig. 6.12a Signal to take the next base.   **Fig. 6.12b**   Signal to round the base.

Fig. 6.12c Signal to stop on the base.　　**Fig. 6.12d** Signal to slide to the right side of the base.

Teaching/Learning Drills

1. To develop competence in coaching the bases, all players should get this opportunity in simulated game conditions. May be incorporated as in team batting drill 5, p. 69.
2. To practice coaching the bases, all players will trade off as coaches and baserunners. Runners line up at home and each will swing at an imaginary pitch and sprint to first base. The coach holds the runner or sends the runner with the appropriate hand and vocal signals. If sent, the runner picks up the third base coach fifteen feet before reaching second. The coach will signal for the runner to hold at second or third, slide or score. The next batter should pick the runner up fifteen feet before home for a slide or stand signal.

Part III
The Defense

Chapter 7

The Battery

The battery pair, pitcher and catcher, are key personnel of a team's defense. All defensive positions are important as it is difficult to "hide" a weak player; however, these two are considered to be the foundation. A team that lacks good pitching, especially in fast pitch play, cannot hope for success over an extended playing season. The catcher, the guiding hand of the defense, is the one who handles the pitcher; a good catcher contributes greatly to the club's defensive success.

The Pitcher

A winning team must have consistently fine pitching, whether in slow pitch or fast pitch softball.Primarily, the pitcher must be able to throw with control as well as making the varied defensive plays that will occur in the game. The fast pitch pitcher must naturally concentrate on developing speed in addition to excellent control. Because pitching is a large part of the game, adequate time must be spent in teaching and improving the pitching staff's varied techniques. Pitchers and those who wish to pitch must be willing to work very hard at mastering the control of several pitches. Additionally, pitchers should develop and display total concentration and self-confidence to become truly effective. There are very specific pitching rules that dictate the positioning and delivery of the pitch. An individual motion that is both efficient and comfortable must be perfected within these restrictions.

CONCEPT I: Proper fundamental mechanics in the beginning positions will yield an effective and efficient pitch.

Key Points: (Fig. 7.1a, b)

1. Grip the ball across the seams in a firm and deep tripod with two or three fingers in opposition to the thumb.

   Increases friction allowing for good force transfer to the target area; allows greater spin to be imparted to the ball, which increases control for varied pitches.

2. Stand in a forward stride position with the rear cleats of the right foot over the front edge of the pitching rubber and the left foot behind the toes in contact with the back of the rubber.

   Establishes a firm reacting surface with the base of support; increases the range of movement toward the target to increase momentum and speed on the pitch.

3. Place the feet a comfortable distance apart, about shoulder width, with the right foot pointing slightly toward third and the left foot pointing slightly toward first base.

   Gives stability and good positioning for the rotation and weight shift needed on delivery.

4. Lean the upper body back slightly while squarely facing the plate with the shoulders.

   Gives added distance needed to increase the velocity or the arch.

5. Bend the elbows with both hands together at the waist, positioned slightly to the throwing side.

   Presents the ball to the batter in a stationary manner.

6. Keep the eyes on the target.

   Helps in the application of force in line with the intended path of the ball.

Fig. 7.1a Basic pitching grip.

Fig. 7.1b Beginning position presenting the ball to the batter.

CONCEPT II: Proper fundamental mechanics in the delivery and follow through will yield an effective and efficient pitch.

Key Points:

1. Move the upper body toward home plate.

   Initiates the necessary weight shift.

2. Rotate the body—right foot, shoulders and hips—even more toward third base and shift the weight back as the hands separate.

   Allows more rotation for greater velocity or arc on the pitch.

3. (Slingshot) Bring the throwing arm back behind the body to full extension with the wrist hyperextended; step toward home and rotate the trunk and shoulders back toward home as the arm comes down and forward with a powerful thrust. (Fig. 7.2a, b, c, d)

   Gives excellent control as the arm motion is grooved.

Fig. 7.2a Beginning to take the ball back in the slingshot delivery above the head.

Fig. 7.2b Bringing the arm back well above the head.

Fig. 7.2c Bringing arm forward just prior to releasing the ball.

Fig. 7.2d Following through.

(Windmill) Bring the arm up over the head and then around and through in a large circular motion close to the body as you step toward home plate. On the backswing the elbow should not be locked, but relaxed to allow for a whipping action as the forward momentum of the entire motion builds. The shoulder must rotate freely throughout the circular motion. (Fig. 7.3a, b, c, d)

Fig. 7.3a Beginning to take the ball over the head in the windmill delivery.

Fig. 7.3b Continuing the large circular motion of the windup.

Fig. 7.3c Preparing to release the ball.

Fig. 7.3d Following through.

Yields greater momentum and increases force and speed though with somewhat less control.

(Figure Eight) Bring the arm back quickly, out and away from the body, extended opposite the hip and then back forward at an angle, in close to the body directly toward the batter.

Increases speed with a possible loss of some control.

(Players should experiment with each style and choose the most natural and comfortable type of delivery.)

4. Move the glove hand and arm in opposition to the throwing arm.

   Yields good balance and stability in the motion.

5. Stride between three and five feet; plant the toes first and point them directly at home plate.

   Stabilizes the body, allowing for more force to be given to the ball; places the pitcher nearer the batter.

6. Cushion the shock of the stride by giving at the ankle and knee.

   Avoids injuries to the foot and knee by absorbing the constant force.

7. Snap the wrist immediately before releasing the ball between the knee and hip for fast pitch and at head level for slow pitch; shift the body weight and stride simultaneously with the snap and release.

   Generates the ball's arch or velocity.

8. Increases speed of the arm and hand as well as the speed of the wrist snap and the rotation of the hips, trunk, and shoulders.

   Increases the velocity of the ball.

9. Move the right foot forward naturally on follow through and assume a ready position with knees flexed.

   Gives an alert position for quick defensive play.

CONCEPT III: Proper fundamental mechanics in the grip and release will yeild effective development of varied pitches.

Key Points:

1. Curve ball—Grip the ball deeply and stretch the fingers across the narrow seam area to impart the necessary spin; snap the wrist forward and to the side you wish the ball to curve upon release; and allow the ball to roll off the fingers in that direction, either left or right.

   Causes the ball to curve in proportion to the air resistance.

2. Drop ball—Grip the ball deeply across the narrow seams to impart the necessary forward spin; snap the wrist on release by removing the thumb from the top of the ball first and spinning the ball forward with the fingers moving upward.

   Causes the ball to drop in proportion to the air resistance.

3. Rise ball—Grip the ball deeply by stretching the fingers across the wide seams on top with the thumb on the botton of the ball (opposite the other two grips); snap the wrist upward on release as the thumb pushes against the ball to impart the necessary backspin.

   Causes the ball to rise in proportion to the air resistance.

CONCEPT IV: Proper fundamentals in the follow through allows an effective pitch and good defensive positioning.

Key Points:

1. Come forward with the standing foot directly toward home with the knee flexed; bring the back foot through to a parallel position with the knee flexed.

   Keeps the body over the base of support and allows quick response for defensive play.

2. Align the shoulders with first and third base by continuing to rotate the trunk to the left while keeping the eyes on the batter.

   Allows for smooth completion of the pitch and gives good defensive position.

   NOTE: Mechanically, the key points as described are quite similar for both the fast and slow pitch. The key points under concept one and four are identical for both styles of pitching. In terms of the delivery described in concept two, the rotation of the body need not be as extensive for the slow pitch as that described for the fast pitch. The arm motion in the slow pitch delivery is straight back and through, quite similar to the slingshot delivery. The basic difference is in the speed of the arm and the point of release, which combine to produce very different outcomes. In order to generate sufficient arch to the slow pitch, the ball is released head high with an extended arm. The motion is fairly slow because a build up in velocity is neither required nor desired, rather the ball must simply drop properly into the strike zone from the peak of its arch. All other key points apply to both styles of pitching; with practice, the varied spins may also be imparted to the slow pitch to produce pitches that will curve or rise and drop more quickly than expected. (Fig. 7.4a, b, c)

Fig. 7.4a Taking a step as the arm comes forward in a slow pitch delivery.

Fig. 7.4b Bringing the ball forward to be released at shoulder height.

Fig. 7.4c Following through.

CONCEPT V: Proper positioning and strategy will yield effective defense by the pitcher.

Key Points:

1. Field all grounders and pop flies within reach forward and laterally by immediately coming to an alert ready position upon completion of the pitch. (Fig. 7.5a, b, c, d)

Fig. 7.5a Beginning to move to a defensive position after delivering a slow pitch.

Fig. 7.5b Standing in a ready position.

a

b

Fig. 7.5c Moving to get in line with the ball.

Fig. 7.5d Reaching to catch the ball.

c   d

Sets up a first line of defense as it closes the middle; offers protection from possible serious injury.

2. Break for the ball as quickly as possible in bunt situations. Field the ball with both hands, pivot and throw hard to the inside of the base. (The catcher will call for the throw to go to first, second, or third base.)

   Gives the most effective play to get the lead runner.

3. Throw accurately to the shortstop covering second base on double play balls. Lead the shortstop just slightly and throw chest high so the relay to first may be made in a continuous motion with no break in momentum.

   Sets up an efficient double play.

4. Move quickly to cover home on any balls that get away from the catcher when runners are in scoring position. Straddle the inside portion of the plate to leave the outside of the plate to the runner. Face the throw and make the tag with the back of the glove on the ground in front of the plate. Do not attempt to block the plate.

   Allows the fielder in the best position to help protect the plate; avoids injury by making the tag and staying out of the way.

5. Move quickly to cover first base on all balls hit to the right side of the infield. Call for the base and anchor yourself to the corner of the base for a stretch in the direction of the throw.

   Keeps first base covered at all times and decreases confusion concerning coverage.

6. Take the position in the infield as the cut-off, twenty feet in front of the plate, both arms up overhead, on balls hit to the

outfield with runners in scoring position. The catcher will call for the cut and throw to the proper base when appropriate or will remain silent if you are to let the throw go through to the plate.

Fig. 7.6 Pitcher serving as the cut-off man on a hit to right field.

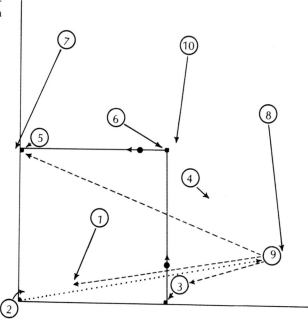

Gives the players with most advantageous positioning the key roles in making a successful play; avoids confusion by designating a single player to take all cut-offs.

7. Back up throws to second or third when runners are not in scoring position. Stay alert and involved in every play.

   Sets up a second line of defense by a player in the most advantageous position.

8. Move quickly to cover third base whenever it is left unprotected with a runner advancing toward it. Talk with the infield in advance of this play possibility to acknowledge your responsibility.

   Keeps the base protected, increasing the chance for a successful play.

CONCEPT VI: Mental preparation and concentration combined with good knowledge will yield sound pitching strategy.

Key Points:

1. Work for excellent control of every pitch.

   Keeps the batter in a defensive position.

2. Concentrate on varying the speed of your pitches as well as moving the ball around in the strike zone while demonstrating an identical motion.

   Keeps the batter off balance.

3. Get ahead of the hitter immediately by making the first pitch a strike.

   Makes the batter more defensive and tentative.

4. Keep the head still with the eyes on the target at all times.

   Facilitates the application of force in line with the intended path of the ball.

5. Throw a pitch just close enough for the batter to swing and connect poorly when the count is two strikes; do not throw a "fat" pitch.

   Tempts the batter with a marginal waste pitch.

6. Throw a pitchout high and outside so that the catcher may throw efficiently to one of the bases in the steal situation.

   Keeps the batter out of the play, giving the catcher a better chance to throw.

7. Learn the strengths and weaknesses of each batter that will be faced over the course of the season. Make your pitches accordingly.

   Combines mental and physical pitching skills.

Teaching/Learning Tips and Drills

1. To avoid injury, pitchers should warm up fully before participating in batting practice or pitching drills.

2. To practice the proper wrist snap, a ball may be wrapped in tape with an eight inch tape handle hanging from it. Pitchers should pair off and practice their correct motion by pitching the taped ball to each other. By holding the tape handle, the wrist must be snapped in order to propel the ball.

3. To practice covering first base, all pitchers will line up on the mound and alternate pitching to the catcher. The coach will

fungo a ball toward the first baseman who will field the ball and throw to the pitcher covering first. This drill can also be adapted to practice covering third by hitting at the third baseman. Both drills can then be combined with the coach occasionally hitting back through the middle to keep the pitcher from starting too soon.

4. To practice backing up the bases and playing the cut-off position, pitchers should assume these duties in a simulated game situation. Runners are placed on specified bases and advance as the hits to varied parts of the field. The pitcher will take the appropriate positioning on each play. The score, inning, and number of outs may be added for realistic strategy decisions.

5. To practice moving quickly from side to side and picking up slow rollers as wells as increasing flexibility, pitchers will pair off about ten feet apart. One will toss thirty grounders to either side of the other. The fielder will make the play by bending deeply at the knees and tossing it back underhand. The distance laterally and the speed of the tosses should be increased. Players will then exchange positions.

6. To practice quickly assuming a defensive ready position, fielding batted balls, and making accurate throws, all infielders will participate. The pitcher makes the pitch to the catcher and prepares to cover defensively. The coach will fungo balls up the middle for the pitcher to field and alternate throwing to first and second base. Each pitcher will field ten balls. Hard grounders and line drives should be included to the extent that the player's skill level is high enough to be fairly successful without becoming injured.

7. To practice charging and fielding bunts and then making hard and accurate throws, drill 5 can be repeated with the coach laying down bunts. Both drills can then be combined and runners added to simulate game conditions. Pop ups can occasionally be hit to keep the runners honest.

8. To develop control of varied pitches, each pitcher should practice with a target on a mat hung from a fence or wall. A bucket, placed at a spot just behind the point of the plate, should be used as the target by slow pitch pitchers. The pitcher will practice alone, concentrating on proper form and mechanics as well as accuracy.

9. To develop control on varied pitches, each pitcher should practice with a catcher by throwing from the proper distance

and over home plate. The catcher will set his mitt as the target inside, outside, high or low, all within the strike zone. One point is awarded for each pitch for which the catcher does not move the target to make the catch. This drill should continue to twenty points.

The Catcher

The catcher should be agile, strong, and always alert. The catcher should act as a leader on the field, willing and able to help direct the play of teammates from the excellent vantage point behind the plate, the only player able to see everyone else on the field at a glance. The catcher must assist the pitcher in handling all batters and is ultimately responsible for the only base where a run may be scored. He helps determine defensive strategy, backs up first base when feasible, and, in fast pitch, keeps the baserunners honest with a strong and accurate arm to cut down potential stealers or bunters. It is recommended that all catchers wear both a chest protector and a mask, not simply to avoid injury but because protective equipment will add to the self-confidence of the catcher in making a tough defensive play at the plate. It is also recommended that a first baseman's mitt be used because the big pocket and long webbing offer excellent control of the ball. This mitt is generally more flexible than a regular catcher's mitt, giving more control for the larger softball. Fast pitch catchers may prefer to use a break-rim. A size should be chosen that the player will be able to totally control.

CONCEPT I: Proper fundamental mechanics in the initial stance and ready position will yield effective reception of pitches.

Key Points:

1. Squat with the feet close together, weight forward on the balls of the feet, while giving signals to the pitcher or when resting between pitches.

   Gives a more restful position while protecting signals from the opponents.

2. Give the signals high and between the legs. One simplified system is one finger for the fast ball, two for the curve, three for the rise, four for the drop, and a fist for the pitchout.

   Makes pitching systematic in avoiding confusion with the pitcher.

3. Take a comfortable and crouched ready position immediately after giving the signal and give the pitcher a target with the mitt about chest high. The weight is forward, hips flexed, feet spread with the left foot slightly ahead, and the elbows as wide as or slightly wider than the knees. (FP) (Fig. 7.7a)

Yields good balance and readiness to move in front of pitch.

or

Remain in the squat position and place the mitt on the ground just behind the plate for the target. (SP) (Fig. 7.7b)

Gives a good balance and a target for the pitcher.

Fig. 7.7a Basic catching position in a fast pitch game.

Fig. 7.7b Basic catching position in a slow pitch game.

4. Take a position as close as possible to the batter without interfering with the swing.

Allows more strikes to be saved by catching the ball directly behind the plate, to receive more balls before they bounce, to catch more foul tips, to be in good position to move out quickly to throw, field bunts, or catch flies.

5. Catch the ball with both hands but keep the throwing hand loosely folded behind the glove with the fingers pointing downward.

Protects the thumb and fingers from injury.

6. Catch all balls higher than the knees with the thumbs together and fingers up; catch low pitches with the little fingers together and fingers down. (FP)

   or

   Catch the ball in the glove on the ground. Do not snatch at it. (SP)

   Yields the most efficient positioning for receiving varied pitches.

7. Relax the hands and give slightly on the catch.

   Absorbs the force of the pitch rather than rebounding the ball stiffly.

8. Focus on the seams of the ball from the pitcher's release to your glove; do not blink.

   Increases the chance of making a clean catch.

9. Block low balls by dropping to both knees in front of the ball. Point the mitt down to help keep the ball in front. (Fig. 7.8a)

   Establishes a large barrier for the errant ball.

10. Keep the body squarely in front of each pitch. Block a ball to the right by dropping to the left knee first; your right shoulder should be angled toward the pitcher with your chest square to

Fig. 7.8a Positioning to block a low traveling ball.

Fig. 7.8b Moving to the right to block a ball.

the pitch. The same procedure in reverse is used to block balls on the left. (Fig. 7.8b)

Keeps the ball out in front rather than having it angle away upon striking the body.

CONCEPT II: Proper fundamental mechanics in the throw will improve defensive play.

Key Points:

1. Grip the ball across the seams firmly.

   Prepares for a quick controlled throw.

2. Push the ball against the mitt with the bare hand to get a firm grip on the ball while both hands come to a throwing position.

   Saves time in gripping the ball.

3. Shift the weight and rotate to the right before stepping to make the overhand throw.

   Permits full use of the body needed for a powerful throw.

4. Step forward with the left foot and point the toes directly at the target.

   Permits full use of opposition to give power to the throw.

5. Take a short step forward with the right foot before stepping forward with the left around a right-handed batter when throwing on a steal. (Fig. 7.9a)

   Gives an open view for a throw to second or third.

6. Take a short step forward with the left foot, step forward diagonally on the right foot, and take another step forward with the left foot to get around a left-handed batter when throwing on a steal. (Fig. 7.9b)

Fig. 7.9a Catcher's foot positions when throwing to second or third bases past a right-handed batter.

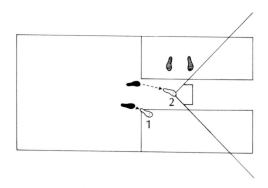

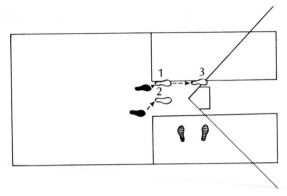

Fig. 7.9b Catcher's foot positions when throwing to second or third bases past a left-handed batter.

Gives an open view for a throw to second or third.
7. Throw knee high, slightly in front of the base on the side from which the runner is advancing.

Forces the runner to slide into the tag.
8. Choose from among the following plays with runners in the double steal position at first and third bases.
    a.   Throw to third if the runner has a wide lead or has started home.
    b.   Look the runner back to third and throw to get the runner going to second; the shortstop will charge to receive the ball in front of second and throw home should the runner on third break for home.
    c.   Look the runner back to third and throw to get the runner going to second; the shortstop will take the throw and make the tag if the runner on third remains stationary.

Gives flexibility to make the appropriate play.

CONCEPT III: Proper fundamental mechanics in protecting home plate will yield effective defense while reducing the chance of injury to any players.

Key Points:
1. Avoid collisions at home by allowing baserunners to slide into the outside portion of the plate.

Prevents possible injury and establishes a position to tag properly.
2. Take a position in front of the inside portion of the plate; face

the throw in a comfortable slight stride position; do not straddle the plate. (Fig. 7.10a)

Yields an effective and safe tag play.

3. Play the ball first, not the runner. (Fig. 7.10b)

Prevents misplaying the ball through distraction.

4. Hold the ball firmly in the bare hand inside the mitt, drop to the right knee, turn to the left and allow the runner to slide into the tag. (Fig. 7.10c, d)

Protects the ball and prevents injury.

Fig. 7.10a Waiting for the throw in front of the plate on the third base slide.

Fig. 7.10b Turning toward the runner after catching the ball.

Fig. 7.10c Beginning to drop low in order to tag the runner.

Fig. 7.10d Reaching to tag the runner.

5. Stand with the left foot on the plate for a forced play when there is a fast runner on second; step with the right foot and then the left into the infield to make the throw to the inside of first base to complete a double play. (Fig. 7.11a)

   Ensures an accurate throw for the second out on the slowest runner.

6. Stand with the right foot on the plate for a forced play when there is a slow runner on second base; step out on the left foot and throw to third base to complete the double play. (Fig. 7.11b)

   Saves the time needed to get the putout on the lead runner.

Fig. 7.11a Positioning feet for a forced play at home when there is a fast runner on second base.

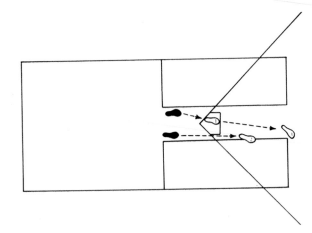

Fig. 7.11b Positioning feet for a forced play at home when there is a slow runner on second base.

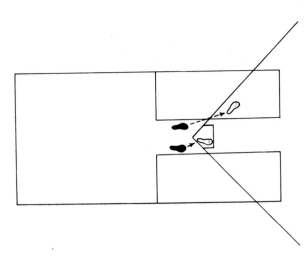

CONCEPT IV: Proper fundamental mechanics in fielding pop flies will yield an effective defense.

Key Points:

1. Catch a short pop fly, whether fair or foul, with both hands above the head. Allow time for the backward drift caused by backspin on the ball.

   Gives more time and flexibility for adjustments that may be needed to make the catch of a spinning ball.

2. Locate the pop up; toss the mask in the opposite direction; move quickly under the ball.

   Prevents stepping on the mask.

3. Yield to any fielder who calls for the ball.

   Gives the catch to the fielder in the best position and with greater experience in catching fly balls.

CONCEPT V: Proper positioning and strategy will yield effective defense during game play.

Key Points:

1. Back up first base whenever a ground ball is hit to the infield with no baserunners or with a runner on first only. Get in positioning behind the throw when possible, but in all cases, be alert for a rebound off the first baseman or the baserunner.

   Prevents runners from advancing on an overthrow.

2. Use two hands in fielding bunts. Scoop the ball into the glove with the bare hand; gain control with a firm grip; make the throw.

   Gives needed control and decreases the probability of a fielding or throwing error.

3. Call out the proper base clearly for the throw on all bunts that are not fielded by the catcher.

   Allows the decision to be made without confusion by the player with the best position and view of the entire situation.

4. Call the play for the infielder in the cut-off situation. Remain silent if the ball is to come through to the plate; call "cut" and the correct base for the throw if there is no chance to get the

runner at home but there is a chance at another base. Make the decision quickly and with confidence.

Allows the decision to be made without confusion by the player with the best position and view of the entire situation.

5. Maintain a good relationship with the umpires; do not quarrel needlessly over calls nor block his vision or distract him with extraneous movements.

Keeps the play smooth while reflecting confidence in the pitcher and yourself and keeps the team in good standing with officials.

6. Run the baserunner back toward third base in a rundown. Make one fake then throw to get the out when the runner is committed and about two-thirds of the way back to third.

Reduces the chances of a misplay and increases the chances of a put out.

7. Scout opposing hitters in their practice swings before the game and in early times at bat in the game to help choose appropriate pitches. Jamming good hitters, that is pitching at their hands, is a good general plan.

Locates the weaknesses of each batter and uses these to an advantage.

8. Watch to make sure that all runners coming home touch the plate.

Increases the chance of a successful appeal play or alert tag to cancel an apparent run.

Teaching/Learning Drills

1. To assume the proper receiving position, use a low stool for the catcher to sit on. Flexibility in the thighs can be developed in this position.

2. To make a catcher aware of how many balls are caught, blocked, or missed, each should be tallied during a practice session.

3. To practice receiving or blocking various pitches, the coach will stand about twenty-five feet from the catcher and pitch thirty balls. Begin with strikes and then throw balls—outside, inside, high, low, and include balls that bounce. The catcher is forced to move quickly into proper position because the distance is reduced.

4. To strengthen the throwing arm, catchers will practice the overhand throw while lying on their backs. To develop the correct trunk rotation and overhand motion as well as strengthen

the arm, catchers will practice the throw from their knees. In each, a partner will begin as close as needed to receive the throw from the back or knees and gradually increase the throwing distance by moving backward. This can be incorporated into the daily warm-up routine.

5. To add motivation to develop a quick release and strong throw to second or third base, time the catcher with a stopwatch from the time the ball hits the mitt until it hits the glove of the fielder covering the base. Challenge each catcher to improve his throwing time.

6. To practice making the tag properly at the plate have:
   a. Runners line up at third base, the coach will hit to the infielders; the runner breaks for home on the hit and the infielder throws to the catcher who gives the runner the outside path home and makes the tag. (Runners can practice sliding.)
   b. Runners line up at second base, the coach will hit to the outfielders, the runner breaks for home on the hit, and the designated infielder takes the cut-off position; the catcher will call "cut" or make the play on the runner coming home.
   c. Runners begin at second and third bases, the coach will scatter hits to all players, the runners will attempt to score on the hit, and the catcher must make or call the appropriate play. Balls should be blocked out front when necessary.

7. To practice making good quick throws to second base, runners line up at first and break on the pitcher's release. Initially, the batter will not swing and the catcher will receive the ball and use proper footwork to make the throw. Upon mastery of this phase, the batter will swing and the catcher will receive the ball to make the play under more realistic conditions. Batters will alternate batting boxes.

8. To practice making a quick throw to third base, runners line up at second and drill 7 is repeated.

9. To develop throwing accuracy and add a challenge that is fun, catchers will throw at a target in front of second base. The target is a glove attached to a supporting stick placed two feet high in front of the inside corner (sliding side) of second. Catchers will alternate firing at the target from receiving position on "go" and receive one point per hit. Backup players will retrieve and the game will continue to ten points.

10. To develop throwing accuracy, repeat drill 9 with the second baseman taking the place of the glove target. This player will position his glove in a stationary manner, and if hit without movement, the catcher is awarded a point.
11. To practice catching foul balls, the catcher will assume the receiving position behind the plate and the coach will hit high fouls from the batter's box. The catcher will toss his mask in the proper direction and make the play smoothly and correctly. Catch ten balls in succession.
12. To practice fielding bunted balls all infielders should participate. Place two balls fifteen feet in front of the plate on each foul line and up the middle; runners line up at home and first base. The pitcher will pitch, the batters will fake the bunt, and the catcher will receive the pitch and roll it toward the screen. The batter calls first, third, or middle and the catcher will charge that ball, field it properly, and make the throw. Runners break on the pitch and the success of the throw will depend on both the speed of the runners and the smoothness of the fielding play. The drill continues until all six balls have been played. The sequence may be repeated.

Chapter 8

The Infield

The primary responsibility of the infielders is to convert a high percentage of their fielding chances into outs. Generally, the infielder is dealing with ground balls and because of the layout of the diamond, all can perform their tasks more efficiently if they are right-handed. An exception is that a left-handed first baseman can get to more balls in the hole between first and second and can throw to the other bases without a pivot. Infielders must also protect the bases and keep baserunners from advancing and scoring.

Defensive positions of the infielders are determined by the particular game situation and the ability of the hitter. The score, the inning, and the speed of the baserunners must be considered in properly aligning the fielders. The infield must play extremely tight (nearer the plate) when a run must not be given up, such as late in the game when a runner on third is the tying or winning run; the infield must move back slightly to double play depth when first base is occupied with less than two out and play at normal or deeper alignment when the bases are empty. (Fig. 8.1a, b) Occasionally, one side of the infield will play deeper than the other; for example, with a left-handed pull hitter up, the right side of the infield may move back while the left side may pull in close. At other times, all may shift to the left but stay at normal depth. In an expected bunt situation, the first and third basemen will move in closer than in an ordinary situation and will be prepared to charge to make the play.

The First Baseman

Some coaches have the mistaken idea that it is strategically sound or at least acceptable to position a large hard-hitting player at first base regardless of defensive skills. The first baseman has many difficult duties to

119

Fig. 8.1a Slow pitch infield positions.

Fig. 8.1b Fast pitch infield positions.

 Normal

 Double Play

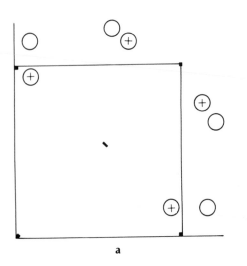

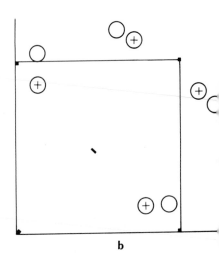

a   b

perform in the course of the game—fielding grounders and bunts, making proper cut-offs and back-ups, initiating double plays, in addition to scooping wild throws from the dirt or leaping for high throws. At the highest levels of competition, a tall left-handed first baseman may be most desirable because the target will be larger and the throw to second or third base can be made without the time consuming pivot needed by a right-handed player. Because the pivot is not necessary, the double play ball or bunted ball is easier for the left-handed player to execute quickly. However, a smaller right-handed player who is quick and agile, with sure hands and the ability to stop most hit balls and errant throws should not be overlooked as a good prospect for this position. The large mitt with its big pocket and long webbing allows for excellent control of the ball, particularly on the one-handed catches that are occasionally necessary. It is strongly recommended that a mitt be used rather than a regular glove and in a size that the player will be able to totally control.

CONCEPT I: Proper positioning will yield efficient and effect play at first base.

Key Points:

1. Play about eight feet deep behind the base and about eight feet in from the foul line (SP) or play about eight feet in front of the base and about five feet in from the foul line (FP) when no one is on base.

   Allows good fielding position for grounders and bunts as well as for a quick but comfortable return to the base to set up and receive throws.

2. Play even with the base and about eight feet in from the foul line with no one on first and two strikes on the batter.

   Covers more area and the chance of a bunt is slim.

3. Play one step in front of the base (out of the path of the runner) and about five feet in from the foul line (SP) or play about sixteen feet in front of the base and about five feet in from the foul line (FP) with first base occupied.

   Yields the best position to get the lead runner at second base.

4. Take a deep position, one step from the foul line and several steps behind the base to protect against the extra base hit late in the game. (A left-handed batter will be more apt to hit the ball down the right-field line.)

   Positions to stop balls going down the line for extra bases late in the game.

5. Consider the score, inning, baserunners, the hitter, and the first baseman's own speed and agility in initially setting up.

   Keeps the positioning flexible and personalized to the situation.

6. Turn and sprint to the base as soon as the ball is hit and then set up to squarely face the infielder in order to receive the throw properly.

   Gives stationary target and makes for an easier catch.

7. Contact the base with the heels without looking down in awaiting the throw. Two different positions for the feet are acceptable.

   a. Start with both heels in contact with the edge of the base. (Fig. 8.2)

   Assures contact regardless of the leg used to stretch for the ball.

   Spread the feet slightly and shift the feet to go for the ball.

   Yields a wide base of support with the ball directly in front of the body.

Reach or stretch to catch the ball with the ball of one foot at the edge of the base. (Fig. 8.2)

Avoids the possibility of being stepped on and gives a longer reach.

Fig. 8.2 First baseman's feet contacting the base before shifting both to make the stretch to catch the ball.

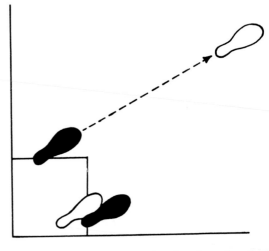

b. Start with the ball of the foot opposite the glove hand in contact with the edge of the base. (Fig. 8.3a)

Yields greater reach but in less mobile and does not allow for last moment adjustments. (Fig. 8.3b)

Fig. 8.3a First baseman contacting the base with foot opposite the glove hand.

Fig. 8.3b First baseman making the stretch too soon.

8. Wait, in either of the described positions; shift, in whatever direction is called for; stretch, only when needed and as far as needed; and catch the ball with two hands. (Fig. 8.4)

Yields best body control and readiness to throw when necessary.

Fig. 8.4 First baseman stretching toward the ball and using two hands to make the catch.

9. Tag the runner in a sweeping motion when contact with the base cannot be maintained due to a wide throw into the base path.

Gives priority to the ball first and then the runner.

10. Give the catcher a target either to the inside or the outside of the basepath when needed. (An inside target would be needed on a short bunt fielded by the catcher; an outside target would be needed on a dropped third strike rolling foul.)

Keeps the throw from being deflected by hitting the runner.

11. Keep the body low rather than upright and keep the head directly behind the mitt rather than turned away for proper sighting on low throws.

Aligns the body with the ball and increases the chance of catching or blocking the throw.

12. Jump vertically for the ball and come down on the base; stand on the edge of the base and reach upward for the ball; or move into foul territory behind the base to stretch for the ball on its way down on high throws.

Ensures the most appropriate action based on the position of the ball and the runner as well as the first baseman's personal skills.

13. Call for and take shallow fly balls behind first base and within

the infield unless called off by the second baseman or right infielder.

Allows the ball to be caught by the fielder in the best position.

14. Step inside the basepath and watch that the runner tags first properly on an extra-base hit or on a tag play. Call for the appeal when appropriate.

Allows the defense to take advantage of offensive mistakes.

CONCEPT II: Proper positioning is needed in fielding ground balls effectively.

Key Points:

1. Assume proper defensive position, get the body directly in front of oncoming grounder, stay low, and block the ball with the body by dropping to one knee when necessary.

Yields greater stability and balance; uses the body as a barrier.

2. Call for and take any and all balls within reach to the right. (The second baseman should be behind as a back-up and the pitcher should cover the base.) Communication is the key to this play.

   a. Throw the ball underhand to the pitcher, not to the base, as soon as possible. The pitcher should start toward first on every ball hit to the right side of the infield.

   Allows the pitcher time to make the catch and then the tag rather than being forced to look for the ball and the base at the same time.

   b. Make an unassisted put-out by calling off the pitcher whenever possible and tag the second base side of the bag.

   Decreases the error possibility on the throw or catch.

   c. Slide straight into the base on extremely close plays.

   Avoids a collision with the runner.

   d. Call for the grounder, "I've got the ball" or the base, "I've got the base."

   Avoids confusion and decreases the chance of error or injury.

3. Decide quickly whether to try for the lead runner at second base or the batter running to first base when fielding a sacrifice bunt or double play ball. The game situation will dictate whether to go for one or two outs. The lead runner is more desirable but

more difficult to get and the speed of both runners as well as the smoothness of the fielding play must be considered.

a. Throw to second with a proper pivot, in an upright position, overhand, and with the opposite foot pointing at the target.

Makes an effective rather than a rushed throw.

b. Throw to first as described in point 2 when unable to get the lead runner.

Ensures an out on the play.

CONCEPT III: Proper positioning is needed to effectively hold a base-runner close to first base.

Key Points:

1. Come back in front of the runner, assume a crouched position straddling the base, and extend the mitt as a target to the catcher.

Helps produce a pick-off with deception.

2. Make the tag by bringing the mitt directly down to the edge of the base and allow the runner to slide or dive back into it.

Avoids missing the runner.

3. Yell "going" when the runner takes off to steal second.

Alerts the catcher and the infielder who will cover second.

Teaching/Learning Drills

1. To master proper footwork on varied throws, another player or coach will stand about fifty feet from the first baseman. This partner will simulate fielding a grounder and throw to the first baseman who starts away from the base, sprints to it, assumes proper positioning, and makes the catch. The partner will move to different fielding positions to give the drill variation.

2. To practice catching all types of thrown balls, a partner will perform the same function as in drill 1. High, low, wide, and in-the-dirt throws should be made to the first baseman. Back-up players should be stationed to retrieve balls that get away in order to keep the drill moving. Runners from home may be added for increased realism and a tag must be made on wide throws in the baseline.

3. To practice pick-off plays from the catcher, runners will be

stationed on first base. The pitcher will pitch to a batter who will not swing and the catcher will fire to first or second—the runner has the option of stealing second or returning to first. To add incentive, a clean steal allows the runner to take a break while an out at either base forces the runner back to the end of the running line.

4. To practice fielding bunts, the entire infield will participate. The coach will bunt towards first, the first baseman will charge the ball, pick it up, and throw to the appropriate base. Initially, this drill is practiced without runners and the ball is thrown to the base called by the catcher. Once this is mastered, the outfielders will run the bases and the first baseman will play the ball as in a game, making the quick decision whether to throw to second or first base.

5. To practice the double play, the same set-up as in drill 4 is used. The coach will hit to the right of the first baseman who will field the ball, throw to second base to the shortstop covering, and then get out of the way for the return throw to the second baseman or pitcher covering first. Runners are then placed on first and second and the throw is to third and back to first.

6. To practice fielding balls in the hole to the right, turning and throwing to the pitcher who is covering, have the right side of the infield participate. The coach will hit into the hole, the first baseman will field the ball as the second baseman backs up the play, and the pitcher will cover first base as a runner runs from home to first. The throw must be directed to the pitcher and not the base.

The Second Baseman

The most important attribute of a second baseman is quickness. Quick hands and feet will help to produce crucial double plays in covering second base and making the relay to first, as well as in covering first in sacrifice situations or other plays initiated by the first baseman. This player must be able to throw accurately from the awkward positions caused by hard, sliding runners bent on breaking up the double play. The second baseman shares several duties with the shortstop—covering second on steals, going out for the relay on extra base hits, and covering second on base hits to the left side. This infielder must have excellent range: forward for slow grounders, backward for shallow fly balls, and laterally for routine as well as hard hit ground balls.

CONCEPT I: Proper positioning will yield efficient and effective play at second base.

Key Points:

1. Play as deep as possible, at least fifteen feet toward first and ten feet behind the baseline, depending on your knowledge of the hitter, when no one is on base. The speed, power, and normal placement of the hitter as well as the condition of the field and the infielder's own ability to move quickly and throw accurately must be considered.

   Allows for good defensive range.

2. Move to double play depth, about three steps closer to home and three steps closer to second base with a runner on first and less than two out.

   Allows second to be covered on a steal attempt, the lead runner to be put out on a grounder, first to be covered on a bunt or ground ball to the first baseman.

3. Move to double play depth and be ready to come in quickly behind the runner on a pick-off attempt from the catcher with runners on second, or first and second, and less than two out.

   Keeps runners close to second base.

4. Move slightly closer to second (the infielder's right) to find the position that allows a play to be made on balls hit to the left. Keep runners on first base from taking third on singles up the middle.

   Extends the fielding range into the more difficult area.

CONCEPT II: Proper positioning is needed to field ground balls effectively.

Key Points:

1. Keep the body in front of the ball and watch the ball without lifting your head.

   Gives a barrier should the ball take a bad hop.

2. Stay low on the ball by bending at the knees rather than the waist.

   Yields a stable body position.

3. Charge the ball and field it with both hands out in front of body.

   Yields an aggressive play that allows the fielder to choose the hop rather than laying back and allowing the ball to play him.

4. Give with the hands by bringing the ball back to throwing position in one continuous motion.

   Yields good control and quick release of the ball.

5. Knock down hard hit smashes that come directly at you (with the glove or body) and make a quick barehanded throw for the out. The body may need to be used because the hop is most difficult to judge in this position.

   Keeps the ball in the infield, possibly giving time for the putout.

6. Field a slow roller with two hands, step and throw sidearm across the body for the out; field the ball barehanded only if it has stopped or is almost stopped.

   Decreases the time to make the throw and two hands gives better control.

7. Pivot on the right foot and cross over with the left to go for balls hit to the right; get in front of the ball if possible, brace the weight on the right foot, turn, and make a strong overhand throw for the out.

   Yields the quickest move to the ball and the proper weight transfer for a powerful throw.

CONCEPT III: Proper positioning is needed in making the double play efficiently.

Key Points:

1. Move to the base quickly and then take a position that will allow you to move to the ball when it is thrown.

   Prevents the misplay that is more likely if the commitment to make the pivot is made too soon.

2. Hit the base with the left foot, push back off it, and make the throw or touch the base and go across it to pivot on the other side to make the throw to first. (Fig. 8.5a, b) The method will depend on the direction of the sliding runner. Be flexible.

   Method one develops quickly but requires a strong arm while method two takes slightly longer but gives greater momentum behind the throw.

Fig. 8.5a Second baseman moves across the base.

Fig. 8.5b Second baseman moves off the base prior to throwing to the first baseman.

3. Assume a first baseman's stretch when the ball is fumbled in the infield or whenever the play will be close at second.

Catches the ball sooner; gets the lead runner for sure.

4. Toss the ball underhanded to the shortstop after fielding a grounder within ten feet of the base. Make the toss firm, without a loop and chest high.

Yields an accurate and controlled throw with a quick release.

5. Tag the base and make the play unassisted when the grounder is within five feet of the base.

Yields a quick play and eliminates timing and throwing errors.

6. Tag the runner and throw to first when the runner is within range.

Yields a quick and efficient play to get both runners.

CONCEPT IV: Proper positioning and strategy will yield effective defense during game play.

Key Points:

1. Go out for the relay on extra-base hits to right field, raise both hands overhead, and call for the ball loud and clear. Make the catch on the glove side and pivot in that direction to make the throw. (Fig. 8.6)

Offers good target and saves time on the throw.

2. Throw to the base indicated by your teammates who will be yelling to you.

Allows players with the best view to make the decision.

Fig. 8.6 Infielder becomes a relay man.

3. Relay the ball quickly to first base after taking the throw at second on a single to the outfield if the runner rounds the base too far and/or turns his back to the ball in returning to first.

   Discourages aggressive turns at first.

4. Call for and take all shallow fly balls behind second base or first unless called off by an outfielder.

   Allows the fielder with the best angle and quickness to field the ball.

5. Step inside the base path and watch that each runner tags second base properly, particularly in tag situations. If not, call for the appeal.

   Allows the defense to take advantage of offensive mistakes.

Teaching/Learning Drills

1. To practice covering and throwing to second base, the coach will hit all types of balls at the infielder. The player will field the ball and throw it properly to the person covering second. Runners from first can be added after the throw has been mastered. The keystone combination (second baseman and shortstop) must become familiar and comfortable with each other.

2. To practice making the double play pivot, the coach will hit grounders to the second baseman or shortstop and these players alternate fielding the ball or covering the base, pivoting, and making the throw to first.

   Sliding players can then be added and both pivots should be mastered to increase the flexible response of the infielders. (Drills 1 and 2 may be combined.) (Fig. 8.7a, b, c, d, e, f)

3. To practice the pick-off play from the catcher, the infielder will receive the throw from the catcher and tag the runner who has led off too far. The pitcher will pitch to a batter who will not swing and a runner will lead off second base. The catcher will fire hard for the out and a sweep tag should be executed. Runners will rotate.

4. To practice tagging out baserunners attempting to steal, the infielder will straddle the base, take the throw, put the glove on the ground in front of the base, and allow the runner to slide into the glove. The coach will throw to second from the pitcher's mound as runners lined up between first and second break for the base. Runners may attempt to dislodge the ball from the infielder's glove. The shortstop and second baseman rotate taking the throw and backing up the play.

5. To practice making accurate underhand throws to second base, the shortstop and second baseman rotate fielding and tossing to second with each taking turns covering the base. The coach will hit to the left and right of second, fairly close to the base, with the infielders in proper position. The fielder should be sure that the glove does not block the view of the ball by the player covering; the glove should be kept low and out of the way.

6. To practice making the play in the hole to the infielder's right, the coach will hit to the right of the second baseman and shortstop while runners sprint from home to first base. The infielders will rotate these plays for at least ten minutes without rest.

7. To practice making the play to the infielder's left, drill 6 can be repeated with the hits going to the left. Both drills should be combined when the crossover step has been mastered.

Fig. 8.7a Shortstop begins to move into position to start a double play.

Fig. 8.7b Second baseman hits the base as the shortstop fields the ball.

Fig. 8.7c Shortstop uses an underhand toss to cover the short distance.

Fig. 8.7d Second baseman moves off the base as she begins to throw.

Fig. 8.7e Second baseman uses an overhand throw.

Fig. 8.7f Second baseman completes the play.

8. To simulate fielding in the fatigue conditions that may occur in the late innings or in double headers, an overload drill can be used. The coach will hit fifteen to twenty-five balls of all types to each infielder who will make the throw to first base and quickly return to ready position for the next ball. A back-up player should be behind the infielder as well as the first baseman to retrieve errant balls and keep the drill moving. Upon completing his fielding, the player will lap the field for added conditioning. This drill should be repeated often.

9. To practice handling all types of hops on grounders and to strengthen the throwing arm, infielders will pair off and bounce the ball back and forth from their knees. Start at fifteen feet and gradually work back to forty feet. This can be incorporated into the warm-ups done daily.

10. To practice fielding the ball in the baseline, place the shortstop, second baseman and first baseman in position and have runners run from first base and home. The coach will hit grounders toward the second baseman who will field the ball, tag the runner, and throw to second (shortstop will cover) and back to first for the double play. This may be repeated for the shortstop to field the grounder, tag the runner going to third, and make the throw to first.

11. To practice defensing the hit and run, place the infield in position with runners at first base. The pitcher will pitch, the runner will break for second, and either the shortstop or second baseman will move to cover. If a right-handed batter hits the shortstop will cover. The batter will not swing but the coach will fungo the ball toward the vacated spot on the infield and the fielder will attempt to recover and make the play.

The Shortstop

The shortstop must be an excellent all-around infielder. This player must have a strong and accurate throwing arm with a quick release and must be able to charge forward quickly on slow rollers or laterally for hot grounders in the hole. The shortstop often handles more balls than the other infielders combined with the possible exception of the pitcher. As with all defensive players, the shortstop should play the hitter according to previous knowledge about power, placement, and speed. Because the shortstop covers such a large area, this anticipation becomes even more crucial. This large area also disallows the luxury of fumbling grounders and recovering to make the play that can be had by other infielders. The shortstop must have the good glove and sure hands needed to field all types of balls cleanly.

CONCEPT I: Proper positioning will yield efficient and effective play by the shortstop.

Key Points:

1. Play about half-way between second and third, slightly closer to second, about ten to fifteen feet behind the baseline with no one on base. Move a few steps closer to third on a right-handed pull hitter. Move in towards the plate on an extremely fast batter. The particular position depends upon the condition of the field, specific knowledge of the batter, as well as the infielder's own ability to move and throw.

   Allows for good defensive range.

2. Move to double play depth, about three steps closer to home and three steps closer to second base with a runner on first and less than two out.

   Allows second to be covered on a steal attempt, the lead runner to be cut down on a grounder, and second to be covered on a bunt or ground ball to the first baseman.

3. Move to a position one step in front of second base on a double steal attempt with runners on first and third. Charge the ball and fire to the plate for the out if the runner on third tries to go home on the throw from the catcher to second. If the lead runner does not break for home, take the throw down from the catcher and make the tag at second.

   Covers several possible situations alertly and aggressively.

CONCEPT II: Proper positioning is needed in making the double play effectively.

Key Points:

1. Move quickly to within a step of the base on the centerfield side with your weight evenly balanced.

   Prevents the misplay that is more likely when the commitment to the pivot position is made too soon.

2. Catch the ball one step in front of the base and then either step with your left foot to the right field side, dragging the right foot

across the base to prepare to throw, or touch the base with the left foot and step back into the infield with the right foot to make the throw on your next step by the left foot. The pivot used will depend on the throw and timing as well as the direction of the sliding runner. Be flexible.

Method one develops more quickly and yields greater momentum behind the throw while method two gives more control and accuracy.

Points 3, 4, 5, 6 are identical to those listed for the second baseman. Please review them.

CONCEPT III: Proper positioning and strategy will yield effective defense during game play.

Key Points:

1. Go out for the relay on extra-base hits to left field, raise both hands overhead, and call for the ball loud and clear. Make the catch on the glove side and pivot in that direction to make the throw.

   Offers a good target and saves time on the throw.

   Points 2 and 3 are identical to those listed for the second baseman. Please review them.

4. Call for and take all shallow fly balls behind the pitcher in left field, or behind third base, unless called off by an outfielder.

   Allows the fielder with the best angle and quickness to field the ball.

5. Cover second base on all sacrifice plays and grounders toward first.

   Keeps the base covered while the second baseman moves toward first.

6. Back-up second base when the second baseman covers on a steal attempt. Back-up third on throws from the catcher.

   Prevents runners from taking extra bases on poor throws.

7. Never quit on a fumbled ground ball. Go after the ball and then look for runners attempting to take an extra base or rounding a base too far. Make a good aggressive throw for the out.

   Increases the chance of getting the out even after an error.

Teaching/Learning Drills (These are identical to those listed for the second baseman. Please review them.)

The Third Baseman

The third baseman must have excellent reaction time, quick movements, sure hands, and a very strong throwing arm. Because sharply hit balls come hard and fast, the third baseman generally has time only for two quick steps to make the play. A quick start is more important than sheer speed on most balls although good speed helps in fielding slow rollers or bunted balls. The third baseman should take all balls within range, going towards second to cut the ball off, as the shortstop will back up the play. This infielder must have both the courage to stand in front of the ball and knock down hard smashes and the agility needed to pick the ball up and throw accurately. Knowing the hitters and anticipating the play will help in covering the "hot corner."

CONCEPT I: Proper positioning will yield efficient and effective play at the third base.

Key Points:

1. Play in a normal position about three steps from the foul line and either even with the bag or at most three steps behind the bag with no one on base. Your knowledge of the batter, condition of the field, and the infielder's own ability to move and throw must be considered. (Fig. 8.8)

   Allows for good defensive range.

Fig. 8.8 Third baseman ready to make a play.

2. Move to double play depth, three to four steps in toward the batter with a runner on first and less than two out. Anticipate the bunt by reading the bat. If the bat is lowered, prepare to charge the ball.

   Allows you to get the lead runner in turning the double play.

3. Take a deep position one step from the foul line and several steps behind the bag to protect against the extra base hit late in the game.

Allows you to stop balls from going through to your right for extra bases although you may give up a single to your left.

4. Make a quick decision whether to charge and field the bunted ball or to return and cover third as the pitcher fields the ball with runners on first and second and less than two out. Remind the pitcher before the pitch to cover third should you be pulled off the base.

Uses good judgement and communication, needed to perfect this difficult play.

CONCEPT II: Proper positioning is needed to field ground balls effectively.

Key Points: (These are identical to those listed for the second baseman. Please review them.) (Fig. 8.9a, b, c, d)

Fig. 8.9a Third baseman moves forward and keeps the glove low.

Fig. 8.9b Fields the ball with two hands.

Fig. 8.9c Moves quickly into position to make the throw.

Fig. 8.9d Takes the ball back to make an overhand throw to first base.

CONCEPT III: Proper positioning and strategy will yield effective defense during game play.

Key Points:

1. Go for any balls within reach to the left by pivoting on the left foot and crossing over with the right foot.

   Gives a continuous throw in the direction of first while the shortstop would have a most difficult pivot and throw from deep in the hole.

2. Field a bunt barehanded only when it has stopped rolling. Place the fingers under the ball for a quick pick up and sidearm throw. The throw is a continuous motion across the body from the correct hand position.

   Takes less time and offers more control than placing the hand down on top of the ball.

3. Call for and take all short flies between home and third base.

   Allows the player with the best angle and quickest start to field the ball.

4. Step inside the base path and watch that each runner tags third base properly, particularly in the sacrifice tag situation. If he does not, call for the appeal.

   Allows the defense to take advantage of offensive mistakes.

Teaching/Learning Drills

1. The drills listed for the second baseman can also be adapted to suit the needs of the third baseman. In particular, drills 3, 4, 8, and 9 should be practiced daily.

2. To practice the play on slow rollers and bunts, four balls will be set down on a line to home plate, spaced ten feet apart. The third baseman will charge the first, field it with two hands and make the throw to second base, and then move quickly to the next ball for a similar play. The third ball is fielded the same way but thrown to first, and the last ball is picked up barehanded and thrown sidearm to first. The sequence may be repeated several times.

3. To practice fielding hard hit grounders and line drives, the third baseman will set up close to the line. The coach will hit hard shots at the player for five to ten minutes without a break and the player will field each cleanly or knock it down to make the throw to first.

4. To practice fielding bunts with the coordination needed between the third baseman and pitcher, all infielders will participate with extra players running the bases. Runners start to first as the pitcher pitches to the catcher. The coach will roll a ball down the third base line or between third and the mound. If the third baseman charges the ball, the pitcher covers third and if the pitcher charges the ball, the third baseman retreats to cover the base. This should be practiced until mastered with runners advancing all the way around the bases.

5. To practice the double play, place the infielders in position. The coach will hit grounders toward third base and if the third baseman fields it within two strides of third, he will tag the base and throw to second or first. If the distance is greater than two strides, he will throw to second to start the double play attempt.

6. To practice fielding grounders between the third baseman and shortstop, place the infielders in position. The coach will hit grounders in the hole and the third baseman attempts to make the play, diving if necessary as the shorstop moves to back up the play. If the ball gets by the third baseman, the shortstop makes the play and throws to first.

Chapter 9

The Outfield

Outfielders must be skilled in fielding all types of balls, have strong and accurate throwing arms, and be able to cover much ground quickly. The opponents must be made wary of taking chances on the base-paths due to the powerful and accurate outfield arms. Scoring will thus be minimized. A weak defensive outfielder who hits well will not often drive in as many runs as he allows to score through poor play. All outfielders must stay alert and be one step ahead of the play, move quickly and properly on every ball hit, and be in good position by playing to the strengths and weaknesses of each batter. Outfielders should use a long fingered glove, in good condition. A glove with a large pocket will help snag difficult catches; the quick recovery of the ball for release is not as crucial as in the infield, where a smaller glove is normally used.

The leftfielder, who will receive a great number of balls and therefore must be a very steady and consistent fielder, may have the weakest arm because the critical throw to third base is quite short. The rightfielder should have the strongest arm to make the long throw to third and keep runners from advancing from first to third on a single to right. In fast pitch, the centerfielder should be the fastest of the three and will take all balls within reach, as well as running to back up plays in the other parts of the outfield. This function is normally filled by the extra fielder in slow pitch who will be positioned flexibly according to the particular batter. The centerfielder in slow pitch may be the weakest over-all outfielder because this player can be covered to some degree by the adjacent fielders.

CONCEPT I: Proper positioning will yield efficient and effective play in the outfield.

Key Points: (Fig. 9.1a, b, c, d, e, f, g, h)

1. Take a comfortable, semi-crouched stance in a slight stride position, toes pointing slightly outward, and with both hands out in front of the body.

   Sets a stable, ready position.

2. Rock forward on the toes on each pitch.

   Overcomes inertia and allows a quick move in any direction.

3. Establish the position according to the strengths and weaknesses of each batter and the particular game situation.

   Prepares in advance for the forthcoming play.

4. Catch routine fly balls just above eye level with both hands on the throwing side of the body.

   Saves time on ensuing throw.

5. Catch balls below the waist with the fingers pointing down and with the little fingers together.

   Gives the most efficient catching position.

6. Take the time needed to make a strong throw from a balanced position.

   Proves more effective than a rushed throw.

Fig. 9.1a Rocking forward on the toes as the ball is released by the pitcher.

Fig. 9.1b Moving toward the infield to make the catch.

a

b

Fig. 9.1c Using two hands to make the catch.

Fig. 9.1d Moving quickly into position to make the throw.

c

d

Fig. 9.1e Continuing to move forward as the ball is taken back.

Fig. 9.1f Planting the rear foot while the ball is continuing to move back.

e   f

Fig. 9.1g Getting into position to use the entire body to make the throw.

Fig. 9.1h Releasing the ball well above shoulder level.

g   h

CONCEPT II: Proper positioning is needed in effectively catching balls on the run.

Key Points:

1. Use the arms to pump in running for balls, do not hold the glove out until just before the catch is to be made.

   Yields greater speed in covering ground.

2. Run on the balls of the feet, not the heels.

   Yields a smooth rather than bouncing effect giving a clear view of the ball in flight.

3. Run quickly to the place where the ball will descend, do not drift but try to be moving forward into all catches.

   Yields good position for last moment adjustments and gives forward momentum to the ensuing throw.

4. Turn in direction of throwing hand side and run for balls hit directly over your head; do not backpedal.

   Yields good balance and speed.

5. Pivot on both feet (first step on left foot for balls to the left and on the right foot for balls to the right) and run for balls hit deep to either side without taking the eyes from the ball.

Yields a balanced and quick start after the ball while keeping sight of the ball.

6. Pivot on the foot nearer the ball and use a cross-over step with the other foot on balls hit on either side and in front of you.

Yields a balanced and quick start after the ball.

7. Run quickly to locate and touch the fence and then come back to catch any fly ball near the fence.

Avoids uncertainty about where the fence is and allows the focus to be on the ball as it descends.

8. Call loudly and clearly for all running catches you will make and continue to call until another outfielder also calls your name.

Decreases confusion and possible missed opportunities due to tentative rather than aggressive plays.

9. Name the base loudly and clearly where the other outfielder should throw when backing up the play.

Allows the player in better position to make this decision.

10. Take all shallow flies within reach by calling off the infielders.

Allows the player with forward momentum to make the catch and throw.

CONCEPT III: Proper positioning is needed in efficiently fielding ground balls and throwing for the putout.

Key Points:

1. Drop to one knee, the one on the throwing side, and block the ball when fielding ground balls with no runners on base. Time is not of the essence in this situation.

Prevents the ball from going through for extra bases.

2. Charge the ball and field it in front of your body, coming up for the throw, with runners on base. Time is of the essence as the runners are advancing.

Prevents the runners from taking extra bases.

3. Back up the infielders in front of you on all ground balls. Stay alert because even the most routine ball may be misplayed or may take a bounce away from the infielder.

Sets up a second line of defense.

4. Throw the ball overhand, hard and low, for a put-out or to the base ahead of an advancing runner when a put-out is not possible.

   Brings the ball back into the infield quickly and allows the ball to be blocked rather than having it sail away.

5. Center your body in front of a ground ball, reach forward to field it, and give with flexible wrists in bringing the ball smoothly to throwing position.

   Allows the body to act as a barrier and absorbs rather than rebounds the force of the oncoming ball.

6. Step directly toward the target on each throw and follow through in that direction.

   Allows a longer more accurate throw.

CONCEPT IV: Proper strategy will yield effective defense during game play.

Key Points:

1. Challenge the batter to hit over your head by playing fairly shallow on all but the strongest opposing hitters. Play the percentages that the average batter is going for the base hit, not the long ball (Fig. 9.2a, b, c, d)

   Takes away normal base hits as the fielder should still be able to run under and catch most long balls.

2. Study opposing batters and baserunners to help you play in good position and make proper throws. Watch the batter constantly rather than glancing at the pitcher in order to react immediately on the hit.

   Dictates the position with flexibility in accordance with the game situation.

3. Move quickly on every hit ball, either to field the ball or to back up adjacent outfielders, infielders in front, or the base to which the throw is made.

   Yields total defense by each team member on every play.

4. Let deep foul flies drop untouched when runners will easily advance and/or score, depending upon the game situation.

   Prevents the scoring of the winning run late in the game.

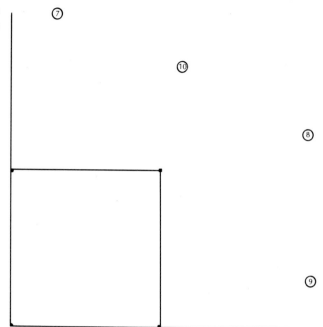

Fig. 9.2a Slow pitch outfielders playing in deep positions.

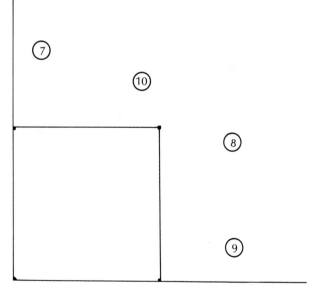

Fig. 9.2b Slow pitch outfielders playing in shallow positions.

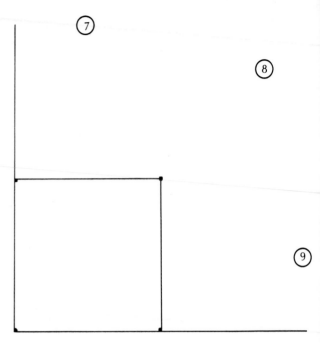

Fig. 9.2c Fast pitch outfielders playing in deep positions.

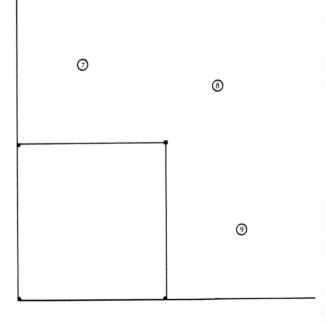

Fig. 9.2d Fast pitch outfielders playing in shallow positions.

5. Expect all balls to be hit to you and know ahead of time where to make the throw in the given situation.

   Develops good anticipation in each player for total defense.

6. Check the direction and velocity of the wind each inning by tossing some grass in the air and make a mental note. Move a step or two in the direction the wind is blowing.

   Prepares for wind effects on the ball, both on the hit and the throw.

7. Check the condition of the field before each game and make mental notes. It may be necessary to block the ball in rough areas or soft spots.

   Prevents both costly mistakes in playing the ball and possible injuries.

8. Check the position of the sun in relation to your field. Shade the eyes with the hand farthest away from the side to which you are running to catch the ball and with the glove hand if the ball is coming in a direct flight.

   Allows the fielder to keep sight of the ball.

9. Make the throw to the proper base according to the game situation: score, inning, number of outs, and speed of the runners. Do not give away extra bases by allowing runners to move up behind a futile throw to the plate when a shorter throw could result in a putout.

   Involves each player in the total defense with alertness and concentration.

10. Throw runners out at first base with a strong and accurate throw on hard hits to right or center field.

    Sets up an unexpected but very possible putout.

11. Throw directly to the glove of the infielder covering second when necessary.

    Gives the accuracy that is most important when baserunners are moving.

12. Throw low and hard to third base, allow the ball to bounce ten to fifteen feet in front of the base if needed.

    Allows the infielder to block the ball and make the tag.

13. Throw at the player in the cut-off position, twenty to twenty-five feet in front of the plate on long throws home. Should the ball go through to the catcher, it will bounce once or it may be caught by the cut-off person and thrown to another base for the put-out.

    Allows the option on the cut-off play.

14. Throw directly to the player in the relay position, chest high, on all deeply fielded balls. Never overthrow the relay by simply throwing as far as possible.

    Makes an effective throw to the relay who will throw for the putout.

15. Hustle immediately after fumbled balls. Worry about mistakes later.

    Returns the ball quickly to the infield.

16. Go all out to make the play on tough chances late in the game when it means stopping the winning or go-ahead run.

    Places you in a "do or die" situation in which you must go for the out or all is lost!

17. Allow a difficult chance to fall in for a single when your team has a good lead.

    Sets up a safe situation to yield a single but deny extra bases.

Teaching/Learning Drills

It is only with much practice and experience that outfielders will learn to get a jump on flies or grounders and move quickly into a good position for the play. Just as much time should be spent in developing skills in the outfield as is spent with skills in the infield. Most of the outfield drills can be done indoors with little or no modification. Distances may be shortened and/or the ball may be thrown rather than batted when necessary due to space limitations.

1. To practice proper footwork individually by each outfielder, the coach will stand about twenty-five feet from the player and throw various types of fly balls in the direction of the player. The cross-step must be used on balls overhead. Corrections for mastery of the footwork should be made immediately.

2. To further practice proper footwork, an alternate form of drill 1 may be used. The outfielder will start even with the coach or partner who tosses the ball out for the player to run down and catch. The fielder must concentrate on watching the ball as well as mastering proper footwork.

3. To practice running quickly to the spot where the ball will descend and preparing to make the catch, the coach or partner will hit or throw fly balls away from the outfielder who will attempt to make the catch behind his back. This calls for complete concentration and presents a real challenge to highly skilled players. The emphasis remains with the quick movement into position rather than on the catch itself. This drill should be used only occasionally for motivational purposes.

4. To practice making accurate relays, all players will participate in groups of five spaced twenty yards apart in a single file. On "go" the ball is thrown down the line from player to player and the group completing the cycle first is the winner. Teams will start over on dropped balls. This drill may be incorporated into the daily warm-up.

5. To practice catching, trapping, or blocking low line drives all outfielders will line up in center field. The coach will stand on the left-field line with a catcher and hit low line drives at each player as they individually charge toward the coach. The fielder will make the play, throw to the catcher on the run, and then veer off to the right to rejoin the group. This is a continuous action drill and each player should have ten chances.

6. To further practice fielding difficult chances, a point system may be added to drill five to increase motivation. One point is given for cleanly fielding a routine fly or ground ball, two points for trapping or cleanly fielding a hard hit line drive, and four points for making a diving or shoestring catch. Two points are deducted for errors and one point is deducted for missing the ball completely on a good effort. The player reaching fifteen points first is the winner. This is a very competitive challenge for high level players as well as for those still developing their skills and can be used for incentive purposes every two or three practice sessions.

7. To improve upon quick movement, endurance, and accurate throws to the bases the outfielder will assume his normal fielding position and the coach will hit twenty to twenty-five consecutive balls of all types at the player from the batter's box. The fielder will make the catch and throw in order to each base; the first ball goes home, the next to third, the next to second, the next to first, and so on. The coach will hit the next ball as the fielder throws the previous ball; there is no rest, this is for continuous action. A back-up player will retrieve any balls hit completely out of the player's range and other players will make the catches at the bases and relay them to the catcher. This overload drill should be performed daily and may be done while another part of the team is on a break.

8. To practice throwing runners out at the plate after a tag play, runners will line up at third base and the coach will hit flies to each outfielder. The runner will break on the catch and the fielder will attempt to throw the runner out at the plate. This may be used for extra incentive in ending a practice session; the runner may be dismissed upon legally scoring and the fielder

dismissed by throwing for the out. Runners and fielders will continue until successful.

9. To increase endurance and practice catching fly balls on the run, all outfielders will line up on the left-field line. The coach will hit each four flies—one each to left, left center, right center, and right field. The hits are consecutive so the next catch will be made on the run. A strong throw home is made after each catch and the player moves quickly for the next ball. When all have completed one cycle and have gathered on the right-field line, the drill is repeated in reverse.

10. To practice throwing hard and low, place the outfielders 100 to 150 feet apart and have them throw one bouncers to each other. The distance may be decreased initially, if necessary. This drill may be incorporated into the daily warm-up.

11. To practice making catches in the vicinity of a fence, all outfielders will move to center field. The coach will throw high flies near the fence and the player will run to find and touch the fence before coming back for the catch. The coach will then hit toward the fence rather than throw. Once this skill is mastered and becomes a habit, this drill need only be repeated occasionally for review.

12. To practice making accurate throws, all players assume their positions. The coach will hit various types of balls to the outfield, beginning slowly and then increasing the pace. Initially, the coach will call the play before the hit for a throw to a base, to the relay, or to the pitcher in the cut-off position. Later, runners are added and the throw must be made properly as under game conditions. This drill should be completed in some form daily.

Chapter 10

Total Defense

      A sound defense is the key to a consistently strong and winning team in softball. All players must be totally alert throughout the game and know, in advance, how to perform in every possible game situation. This can only be accomplished through practice and experience. Major defensive breakdowns generally come when players panic and do not perform in the game as well as they are capable of performing. Hurried or off-balance throws, throws to the wrong base, or being out of position on a crucial back-up play can increase the opportunities for a scoring attack by the offensive team. Concentration during practice sessions as well as in the game will combat these mental mistakes, though physical errors will still occur occasionally. The team should strive to perform as a well-coordinated unit at all times. A team that is not scored upon cannot be beaten. Many scoring threats can be erased by a thinking team.

CONCEPT I: Proper positioning and strategy are needed to yield effective defense in certain situations.

Key Points:

1. The tag—the defensive player should straddle the base, catch the throw with both hands and make the tag by placing the back of the glove between the runner and the base. The runner will be forced to slide into the tag. A sweep down for the tag may be used but lunging for sliding runners is dangerous and could allow the runner to get under the tag and be called safe.
2. The rundown—whenever a runner is trapped between the bases, the defense should take full advantage and make the out easily and calmly. The runner should be forced back toward the base he left and no more than two throws should be necessary to

make the out. The defensive player must force the commitment from the runner by running hard at him with the ball held in a high throwing position. A good fake may deceive the runner, cause him to change directions and run right into the tag. Never throw across the basepath; stay on one side and throw down that side so the ball will not be deflected by hitting the runner. After the throw, move out of the basepath quickly and retreat to the end of the line of those players backing you up. Two or three players should be available, though not normally necessary, at each base during the rundown. These players must be careful to stay out of the play until needed. (Fig. 10.1)

Fig. 10.1 Making a play on the runner caught between the bases.

3. The appeal—whenever a runner leaves a base too soon on a tag-up play or misses a base completely, an appeal to the umpire must be called for by the defense. Time must be in during an ap-

peal play; therefore, the ball must be put back into play by the pitcher. The pitcher will step on the rubber, present the ball to the next batter and then either throw to the base in question or walk the ball to tag the runner. The appeal will be made verbally to the umpire, example, "The second runner missed third base." The ball is on third at this time for the call. Runners may advance at their own risk during the appeal as time is in and the defense must be alert to protect against this.

4. The back up—every play must be backed up, the thrown as well as the hit ball. Outfielders will move to back up the ball whenever it is hit to an adjacent area or move to back up the closest base. Infielders will move to back up the ball when it is hit to an adjacent area unless a runner is advancing toward their base and, in that case, the base must be given first priority. The catcher will back up first base with no runners on or a runner on first only. (Fig. 10.2a) The pitcher will move to the cut-off position when needed or move to back up second or third. (Fig. 10.2b) Team defenses dictates that every player move on every hit according to the unique game situation.

5. The bunt coverage—the first baseman, third baseman, catcher, or pitcher will field the bunt. Base coverage and back-up strategy will vary with the situation. With a runner on first, the

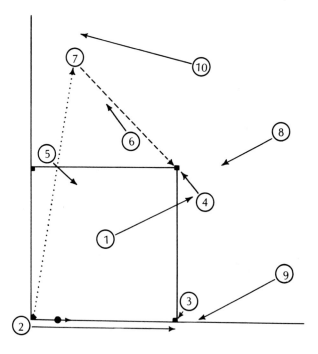

Fig. 10.2a Catcher backing up a play at first base.

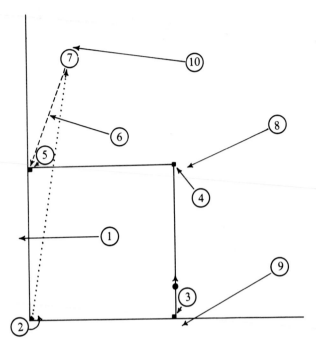

Fig. 10.2b Pitcher moving to back up the play at third base.

defense moves to the right side of the diamond. (Fig. 10.3a) With runners on second or first and second, both sides of the diamond must be covered. (Fig. 10.3b)

6. The cut-off—the first baseman, third baseman, or pitcher will be the cut-off man. A player should be designated for this role in order to avoid confusion. On many teams the pitcher is selected to take the position on all plays necessitating this type of defensive maneuver. (Fig. 10.4a) The first baseman or third baseman assumes this role on other teams. (Fig. 10.4b, c)

Teaching/Learning Drills

All drills should be performed enthusiastically by all players and coaches in order to be most productive. The coach must judge the mixture and length of each drill according to the needs of the particular players on the team and the team as a whole. Maximum participation by all players should be stressed throughout the practice.

1. To practice backing up properly and moving on each hit ball, all players will take their positions. No ball is used; the coach will give a particular game situation and then call and point to where the ball is hit. All players will react and move quickly to their

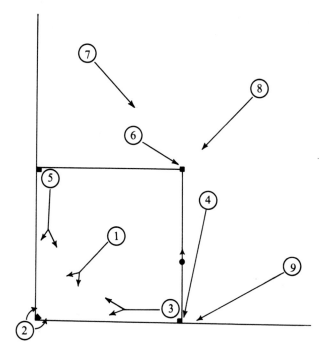

Fig. 10.3a Bunt coverage with a runner on first base.

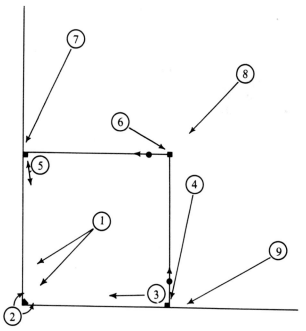

Fig. 10.3b Bunt coverage with runners on first and third bases.

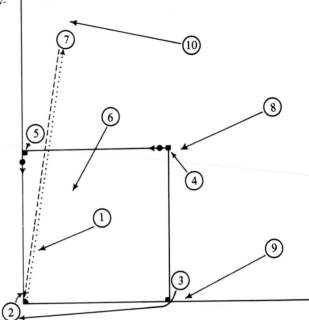

Fig. 10.4a Pitcher moving into the cut-off position.

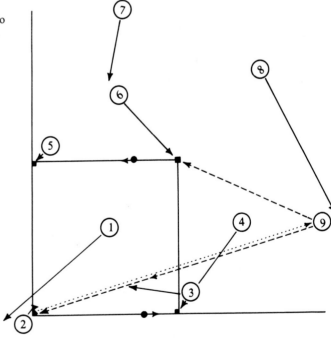

Fig. 10.4b First baseman moving into the cut-off position.

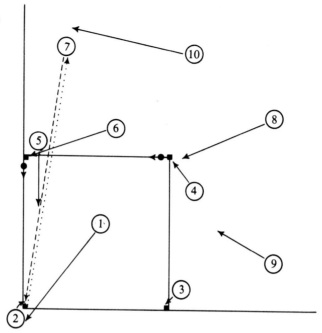

Fig. 10.4c Third baseman moving into the cut-off position.

proper positions. Corrections and reinforcements should be made immediately by the coach. A questioning approach may be incorporated to test knowledge and strategy.

2. To further practice backing up various plays, drill 1 may be repeated with game conditions. The coach will give the situation and then hit anywhere on the field; all players will move to their proper positions for the play and back up. Runners will start from home on each hit and advance as in game conditions. Corrections in positioning or on the throw should be made immediately by the coach.

3. To continue to practice various fielding and back up positions, drills 1 and 2 may be combined with extra players taking turns hitting live pitching and running on each hit. Continuous action can be structured by allowing only one pitch per batter. The number of outs may be varied before rotating offensive and defensive players.

4. To practice defense in a competitive game situation, three teams players will form groups of four (hitter, catcher, fielder, back up) and move to an open area of space. The first batter fungoes twenty grounders at the fielder at various speeds and lateral distances. The fielder makes the play and quickly throws to the

catcher. The next ball is hit immediately. Players rotate to all four positions. The second time through the sequence, line drives are mixed with fly balls. The fielder does not stop at twenty until a final tough catch is made as judged by the other group members.

5. To practice general fielding and throwing accurately to the bases, one player will fungo to the left side of the infield while another fungoes to the right side. The hitter on the left stands in the left batter's box with a catcher and all throws from this side go to third base or home. The right side hitter is stationed on the first baseline with a catcher and throws from this side go to first or second before being relayed back to the catcher. (Fig. 10.5)

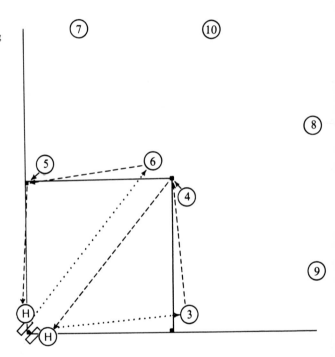

Fig. 10.5 General fielding and throwing drill.

6. To practice defense in a competitive game situation, three teams of five players will compete against each other. Two teams combine on defense, taking the regular positions, while the third team bats. Three outs per inning are allowed by the number of innings may be varied before rotating the groups. An extra challenge may be added to produce runs. Any team that is shut out will run a designated distance upon completion of the game.

Players also serve as base coaches and determine the batting order. Teams should be mixed by position to cover both infield and outfield adequately and offensive power should be equalized as much as possible. The coach may have the teams divided in advance or the players may form their own teams on the spot.

7. To help develop total team defense, all players will take their positions. The coach will give particular game conditions and place extra players on the bases. The coach will then hit live pitching to various parts of the field and the defense must move as a unit for good positioning in making the play. Troublesome plays should be corrected and then repeated.

8. To practice stopping a crucial run from scoring, runners are placed at different bases. The coach will hit:
   a. Fly balls to the outfield; the proper throw must be made after the catch; cut-off and appeal plays will be practiced.
   b. Grounders to the outfield and a quick, yet smooth pick up must be made with a strong throw to the plate.
   c. Grounders to the infield; the proper throw must be made to cut off the score at the plate. (Fig. 10.6)

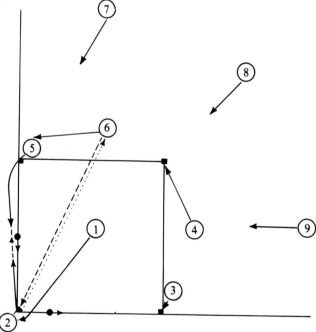

Fig. 10.6 Making a play on the runner moving from third base to home on a ball hit to an infielder.

9. To practice fielding grounders with great concentration, infielders will take their positions and outfielders will retrieve errant balls. The coach will fungo two consecutive grounders around the horn—third, short, second, and first. The third baseman makes the throw to first and goes for the double play to second on the second ball. The first baseman will return each ball to the catcher who feeds the balls quickly to the coach. The shortstop throws the first ball to third, where it goes around the horn. His second throw goes to second base. The second baseman makes his first throw to third; the ball is then thrown around the horn. His second throw goes to the shortstop covering second who throws to first to complete a double play. The first baseman makes the first throw to third; the ball goes around the horn again. He makes his second throw to the plate. This is a most challenging exercise for the players as well as for the coach. Timing is crucial, an occasional pause may be needed until smoothness is developed in the routine.

10. To practice the rundown play, set up the situation between each pair of bases and have the infielders make the play with proper positioning and back up. An extra player, preferably one who is speedy and knowledgeable, will run between the bases. The play should be completed with a maximum of two throws. Corrections should be made immediately by the coach.

11. To strengthen defensive skills in an overload situation, one player at a time will participate with the coach and a back up. The coach will fungo twenty-five consecutive balls at and around the fielder in his normal position. The throw from the fielder is made to a designated base.

Part IV
The
Organization

Chapter 11

Conditioning

Conditioning or training programs are used in all sports. Softball is no exception but it is different from other field sports in that the offensive and defensive moves do not involve direct maneuvering against the opposition as do such games as soccer, field hockey, or football. To play the game well one needs to have a high level of general conditioning and physical fitness, but not the same degree as for other field sports. A player needs to be agile, quick, coordinated, and flexible. He needs to also have a good sense of balance, eye-hand coordination, muscular strength, and speed. However, muscular endurance and cardio-respiratory endurance may not be as essential bscause the action in a game generally covers short distances and is limited in duration. A trip around the bases involves running less than 100 yards; an outfielder backing up a fellow outfielder may need to sprint 30 yards; a fielder may throw the ball 180 feet. The action then ceases and the players rest for a short time before the play resumes.

Offensively, all players need the power to hit and the speed and power to run. Defensively, the physical needs vary with the position being played. A fast pitch pitcher must have high level of muscular endurance in the legs as well as in the arm and shoulders in order to effectively pitch the ball at a high rate of speed for seven innings. The first baseman will need to be much more flexible in order to stretch for the incoming throws. The shortstop covers more area than the third baseman and has to make longer throws so a stronger arm will be needed as well as a quicker release and speed to cover territory. The second baseman does not have to have a strong arm when compared to other infielders. Three outfielders of a fast pitch team each have to cover more territory than the four outfielders of a slow pitch team. However, more balls may be hit to the outfield during a slow pitch game than in a fast pitch game so the outfielders would be involved in more plays and the conditioning needs could be the same.

Not only should one look at the conditioning program in terms of the physical requirements needed to develop better playing skills but also in terms of injuries, as a well-conditioned player is less likely to be hurt. It is much more sensible to condition players to prevent injuries than to recondition players following an injury.

The primary factor to be considered when designing the program is "what are the objectives of the total program?" A highly organized team, such as a varsity, semi-professional, or professional team, usually has winning as the first objective and in order to win, a team must have highly skilled players in very good condition. However, the team in physical education class or in some recreational leagues may have fun and social interaction as the primary objectives. These could be met by players with low levels of general conditioning and playing skills.

The time factor is another element that should be considered. Total time each day for a class is about fifty minutes. Students are given time to dress for the class (5-10 minutes); the teacher checks roll and/or gives the instructions for the period (5-10 minutes); time may be used for an exercise or a warm-up (5-10 minutes); the students drill and/or play the game (20-25 minutes); the teacher reviews the day's work (2-3 minutes) before it is time to dress for the next class (5-10 minutes). Multiply the 20-25 minutes used for drills and/or play each day by 20, the number of days in a four weeks unit, and that equals 400-500 minutes or 6.6-8.3 hours. This is not much time and the emphasis—whether on skill development or general game play—will depend upon the philosophy of the teacher.

A highly organized team that is serious about playing well enough to win will spend this much time on the practice field in three or four days. The coach has more time to spend on the drills needed to improve the players' game skills and the conditioning program that is necessary to improve these skills. If a team practices six days a week for two hours each day over a period of two months prior to the first game, the coach has ninety-six hours, approximately ninety more than the teacher, to develop and improve the players' conditioning and skill levels.

The Highly Organized Team

Off Season

It is difficult to pinpoint the months of the off season because competitive seasons vary. The professional teams and many semi-professional teams play during the summer (May-August). Intercollegiate teams usually schedule games to be played during the late winter and spring (February-May) while the interscholastic teams play during the fall (September-October) or spring (March-May). Recreational leagues may be active in the north only in the summertime but the southern leagues schedule play from early springtime until late fall.

The off-season months may not be easily identified, but the term off season simply means that time between the end of the regular playing season and organized practice sessions for the next playing season. During this time players may be actively engaged in another highly organized and/or vigorous sport that helps them maintain a high level of general conditioning. If not, they should get involved in a sport that will give them an opportunity to enjoy participating in a different game as well as help them stay physically fit. Swimming, jogging, handball, racquet sports, soccer, and basketball are some of the activities that would be beneficial to play. The racquet sports are especially good because they are vigorous, require body movements similar to those in fielding a ball, and involve striking a moving ball with a racquet.

These types of activities should be supplemented with weight training (the lifting of light weights to improve muscular endurance and heavy weights to build muscle strength) and running programs (sprinting short distances at about 4/5 maximum speed). During this time the bat, ball, and glove should not be stored but used periodically to sharpen the skills specific to the game.

Preseason

This phase of the season begins when the coach thinks that it is time to begin organized practice sessions and/or the league rules dictate that it is time. If the preseason begins several months prior to the opening game, practices may be scheduled for every other day. Work in the early part of this phase should involve the development of muscle strength, the specific skills of running (acceleration, speed, and some endurance), and the specific skills of playing (batting, catching, throwing, fielding).

Muscular Strength

To develop the muscles an exercise program should be designed to condition the total muscular system. In addition to a weight program, general calisthenics should be included. Flexibility exercises, using fluid and not ballistic movements, are vitally important. To stretch the muscles in the chest, shoulders, and upper back, do arm flings, arm circles, prone elbow lifts, and the swimming back stroke. Exercises such as the trunk twist, lateral stretch, leg overs, and twist and bend will loosen the muscles in the trunk area. Toe touches, hurdle sits, knee-to-nose kicks, and high kicks will tend to make limber the muscles in the lower back and legs. Exercises to develop abdominal strength (such as sit-ups and roll downs), coordination (such as jumping jacks and rope jumping), and agility (such as rope jumping and shuttle runs) are also of great value to the player.

Muscular strength is developed by the use of high resistance (a heavy weight of at least two-thirds maximum) and low repetitions (1 to 15 times) while muscular endurance is developed by the use of low resistance (a light weight) and high repetitions (at least 100). If one chooses to develop moderate strength and moderate endurance, an in-between weight and in-between number of repetitions should be utilized.

When executing plays, a player generally combines muscle strength with speed—the bat is brought around rapidly to strike the ball, the arm moves forward at a fast rate to propel the ball across the diamond, the fielder moves quickly across the field, and the baserunner accelerates as the base paths are traveled. In order to meet the specific need for performing different plays the conditioning program should combine the development of strength and speed. Many coaches use types of isokinetic machines, such as pulley weights or Exergenies, that apply resistance while permitting the player to move through a full range of motion needed to execute a specific skill. A body conditioning program for baseball players that may also be utilized by softball players, using the Exergenie has been developed by Tuckett and Law.[1]

Running

Jogging can be used for a warm-up or endurance activity, but players must run sprints (30-40-50 yards) with the accent on acceleration as well as speed. Check the time needed to cover the set distance as well as the time for the first five or ten yards. To make the activity more specific to the task, spend time running the bases. Quick starts are important so work should be done on taking the first step as soon as possible. Give a visual stimulus, such as hand movement or ball release, and note how quickly the player takes the first step.

Specific Skills

All players should be involved in the skill development phase. Select drills designed to improve the specific skills needed for specific situations. A player must work on the skills as well as the muscles that are needed to play the game. Infielders will have to catch many ground balls but not as many fly balls as the outfielders. Outfielders must spend time both catching all types of fly balls and fielding ground balls. The pitcher must work with the

---

1. Tuckett, G. and Law, V. *Ten Station Circuit for Baseball.* Fullerton, Calif.: Exer-Genie, Inc., 1970.

catchers who must have time to practice catching pop ups, fielding bunts (fast pitch), and throwing. Throwing, for power and accuracy, should take much time, and batting practice is essential. In a practice session, batting should receive the greatest amount of time. A typical practice session would include:

Activity	Time Allotment
Stretching Exercises	5-7 minutes
Sprinting	5-18 minutes
Skills Specific to the Game	75 minutes
Strength	15 minutes

Season

League play begins. The number of games per week and per season will vary among the leagues but regardless of the playing schedule, the emphasis moves farther from conditioning to the development of team defense and refinement of the individuals' skills. Approximately twenty-five percent of the practice time should be alloted for warm-ups. Hopefully, the players are in good condition and what they need at this time is the loosening-up drills to prevent injury, drills to maintain physical conditioning level, as well as general drills for skill development.

Players should do exercises each day and particular emphasis should be given to the stretching and running exercises. The first part of each session should be the time to "loosen-up"; other conditioning drills can be incorporated into other phases of the practice. Base running and other offensive play can be combined with team defense drills. Outfielders can practice their sprinting by catching fly balls hit away rather than to them. Infielders can get a good workout by fielding and throwing innumerable balls. Many coaches, even though the workout has been strenuous, will have the players run sprints at the end of the practice.

During this competitive phase it is important to remember that maximum workouts should not take place the day before the game. The number of hard workouts per week will depend upon how many games are scheduled. Players cannot play well if they have not recovered from participating in strenuous practice sessions.

Class Teams

Conditioning is not generally a primary objective of the softball player in a physical education class. The interest of the participant is usually centered on playing the game rather than on getting in condition to play.

The periods are too short to develop a high level of both skill and physical fitness.

However, the teacher should be concerned about the students' condition. The development of skill is generally an objective of a class as well as the development of fitness. It should be remembered that a well-conditioned player is not as likely to get hurt as an individual in poor physical condition. A player can pull a muscle while running in a class or develop a sore arm from throwing as well as one can on a highly organized team. Fingers can be sprained or broken, the body bruised, or the skin lacerated on any field in any league.

If the students have been participating in a prior activity that has required them to sprint, use arm and shoulder muscles needed to throw, be loose and flexible—then they will be in condition to play a game in class. Some type of exercise should be included to help them maintain a level of conditioning, because merely playing a softball game in class will not give them the needed activity. If they are not in reasonably good condition, emphasis should be on developing their overall condition. Students should be taught to handle their bodies before being given a bat and ball. If nothing else is done, have the players begin throwing short distances and progressively increase the distance, easily and not overpowering their teammates. They should run at half-speed prior to running the bases at full speed.

The development of physical conditioning should not be isolated from fundamental techniques and playing tactics. Development of an individual's playing skills and general conditioning and a team's offensive and defensive tactics can be developed concurrently. It is not impossible to achieve many objectives—skill development, physical fitness, pleasure, acceptable behavior—in a well-planned program. Often times it is not the amount of time given to something but how well that time is used.

A class team has a preseason and a season as does the highly organized team; the big difference is that the time period is much shorter for the students. Two weeks, in a four weeks unit, may be allotted for the preseason leaving two weeks for the playing season.

Preseason

This time period begins when the teacher decides that it is time to start the softball unit. Ways to determine the entering fitness and skill levels of the students include: knowing their activity background for the past years as well as the current one, watching them perform skills specific to the game, and giving an entry test. The program should begin at entry level of the student.

A typical class could be divided into time periods similar to a team practice session.

Activity	Time Allotment
Warm-up exercises	5 minutes
Sprinting	5 minutes
Skills specific to the game	25 minutes

Warm-up Exercises

Use the overload principle. Begin with a low number of repetitions (10-15) or short periods of time (20 seconds). Gradually increase the number of repetitions and/or the time length. The speed of each repetition could also be increased. There are innumerable exercises to be done; make sure that all body parts, the limbs and trunk area, are involved. A typical five minute session could include:

Neck Rotation (page 169)
Shoulder Stretches (page 169)
Toe Touches (page 169)
Lunge and Stretch (page 169)
Trunk Rotation (page 170)
Arm Circles (page 170)
Bent Knee Sit-ups (page 171)
Lateral Jump (page 170) (a line can be drawn to replace the rod).
Push-ups (page 170)

Sprinting

Do not have the students run at full speed unless they are properly warmed-up; the speed and/or distance can be increased over a period of time. A progression in a five minute session could be to:

1. Jog the bases slowly.
2. Jog the bases (1/4 speed).
3. Run to first (1/2 speed).
4. Run to first and second (1/2 speed).
5. Run the bases (1/2 speed).

Specific Skills

The basic skills would need to be mastered to a degree of proficiency. Generally, the great joy is in hitting the ball, but oftentimes in class there are too many students in too little space with too little time to spend on this skill. Throwing, catching, and fielding drills can accommodate a greater number in a limited space. Progress from the short distances between the throwers/hitters and catchers/fielders to the longer distances. There may be no need to be concerned with throws covering long distances because a relay person can be used to get the ball in from the outfield.

Season

The emphasis will shift to playing. The ten-minute warm-up/jogging period may be replaced by a skill drill warm-up. The students take five to ten minutes to throw the ball around, field grounders, and run the bases. That leaves twenty-five minutes, if everything is highly organized, to play a game.

OFF-SEASON GENERAL CONDITIONING PROGRAM*
FIRST THREE WEEKS (perform every day)

Flexibility Exercises

1. Neck Rotation (3 sets of 5)
   a. Pull chin to chest.
   b. Pull chin to right shoulder.
   c. Push chin up and back.
   d. Pull chin to left shoulder.
2. Shoulder Stretches
   a. Extend arms sidewards and hold parallel to the ground (3 sets of 10).
      (1) Attempt to touch hands behind upper back.
      (2) Scissor arms in front of chest, move the right arm as far left as possible and the left arm to the right.
   b. Extend arms above head and reach high for the ceiling, extend from tip toes. Hold 5 seconds, relax, repeat 5 times.
3. Toe Touch (3 sets of 10)
   Place feet about 6 inches apart, keep knees firm but not rigid, touch toes with finger tips or palm of hand. Relax 5 seconds between sets.
4. Lunge and Stretch (2 sets of 10)
   a. Stand with feet together, then move right foot to the right 3-4 feet, toes pointed to the right, right knee flexed. Transfer weight from left foot to right foot, keep right knee over right foot. Weight is transferred back and forth between the feet.
   b. Same as the above but to the left.
   c. Move right foot forward 3-4 feet and transfer weight between the feet.
   d. Same as the above but the left foot is forward.
   e. Spread feet as far as possible sideward, grasp ankles and attempt to touch your nose to the floor between your feet.

---

*Arrants, S.L. and Jones, B.J. "General Conditioning Program for Athletes," Unpublished paper, Florida State University, Tallahassee, 1974.

5. Trunk Rotation (1 set of 20)
   a. Extend arms sideward, keep at shoulder level, rotate the trunk of body, keep hips as parallel as possible.
6. Arm Circles (1 set of 40)
   a. Extend arms sideward at shoulder level, rotate arms forward, begin with small circles and increase to large ones. Shake out arms.
   b. Same as the above but rotate arms backward.
7. Elevated Leg Stretch (2 sets of 10)
   a. Place right foot on object so that leg is extended and parallel to the ground, keep left foot planted firmly. Place nose to knee of elevated leg, touch finger tips to toes of same leg.
   b. Touch toes of left foot.
   c. Same as the above but elevate other leg.

Mile Run
   1. Jog 1 mile, take a maximum of 12 minutes.
   2. Repeat flexibility exercises 3 and 4 (1 set of each).

Finger-tip Push-ups (3 sets of 10)
   1. Push-up from finger-tips and knees or feet.
   2. Between sets grasp hands into a ball shape, then spread forcefully.

Lateral Rope Jump (3 sets of 10)
   Place a small rod (that can be displaced easily) a minimum of 6 inches off the ground. Stand to the side of the rod and spring from both feet, jump sidewards back and forth over the rod. Rest 10 seconds between sets.

Ball Squeeze (3 sets of 20)
   Hold a tennis ball in each hand, squeeze rapidly and forcefully. Relax 5 seconds between sets.

Sprints (1 set of 4)
   Sprint 50 yards at 3/4 speed, walk back. Walk for 1 minute after completing set.

Rope Jump (1 set of 1 minute each)
   1. Run in place at a fast pace, pass rope under feet with each step.
   2. Spring jump from two feet as high as possible. Pass rope under both feet with each jump.
   3. Skip rope.
   4. Stretch out after completing set (1 set of 10).
      a. Sit with legs spread in a V shape. Touch nose to knee and fingers to toe of right leg.
      b. Same as above to left leg.

      c.   Stand, cross right ankle over left ankle, touch toes.

      d.   Same as above to left.

Bent Knee Sit-ups (3 sets of 20)

    Lie with feet placed about 12 inches from buttocks, cross arms over chest. Relax 5 seconds between sets.

Vertical Jump (3 sets of 10)

    Place a target 18-30 inches higher than you can stand and reach. Use a two foot take off, jump vertically continuously, attempt to touch target with both hands. Relax 10 seconds between sets.

Flexibility Exercises (Repeat 1 set of each)

FOURTH-FIFTH WEEKS (perform every day)

Flexibility Exercises

    1. Increase range of movements.

    2. Increase number of sets performed by 2.

Mile Run

    Take a maximum of 10 minutes.

Push-ups

    1. Do at least 1 set from finger-tips and toes.

    2. Do 5 sets.

Lateral Rope Jump

    1. Raise the rod 3 inches.

    2. Do 10 continuous jumps without missing.

Ball Squeeze

    Increase to 5 sets.

Sprints

    Increase to 6 sprints at 4/5 speed.

Rope Jump

    Add 1 minute of spring jumping.

Sit-ups

    Increase to 4 sets.

Vertical Jumps

    Increase to 4 sets.

Flexibility Exercises

    Do 1 set of each.

SIXTH WEEK (perform every day)

Flexibility Exercises

    1. Neck Rotation (5 sets of 8)

    2. Shoulder Stretches

      a.   5 sets of 15

      b.   10 sets of 5

    3. Toe Touch

      5 sets of 15

4. Lunge and Stretch
   4 sets of 15
5. Trunk Rotation
   3 sets of 20
6. Arm Circles
   3 sets of 60
7. Elevated Leg Stretch
   4 sets of 15

Mile Run
> Take a maximum of 8 minutes.

Push-Ups
> 5 sets of 10, at least 2 sets from the finger-tips and toes

Lateral Rope Jump
> Raise height of rod 3 inches

Ball Squeeze
> 5 sets of 30

Sprints
> 8 at 4/5 speed

Rope Jump
> Add 1 minute to skipping

Sit-Ups
> 4 sets of 25

Vertical Jump
> 4 sets of 15

Flexibility
> 1 set of each

Chapter 12

Coaching

There is a coach, oftentimes several coaches, for each team. The ASA estimated that there were more than 860,000 teams in recreation, school, armed forces, and ASA leagues in 1975. This indicates that there were over one half-million coaches—a half-million individuals engaged in similar tasks, striving to reach comparable goals. One common goal is to be considered a "successful" coach, though all do not try to reach this goal in the same way.

There is no magic formula for becoming a successful coach. Those who are thought to be successful (the definition of what is successful is highly debatable) have come in many shapes and sizes, from varied backgrounds, with different skill abilities, and with unlike philosophies. There are many who believe that there is one common denominator—that of being a good teacher. Having a thorough knowledge of the rules, fundamentals and strategies and/or the ability to play the game is of little use if the material cannot be presented in such a way that the player understands, learns, and is motivated to perform to his maximum potential.

Coaches are usually more fortunate than teachers in that their students are fewer in number and want to be a part of the team. However, coaches should be as conscientious and systematic in planning their program as any good teacher. The competencies, both professional and personal, of the two roles run on a parallel, if not identical, track.

The Coach

What personal qualities should the coach have? There are many that would be assets including being energetic, enthusiastic, decisive, fair-minded, intelligent, and people-oriented. It would also help to have a good sense of humor, the ability to analyze, good mental and physical health, a respect and appreciation for the individual, and leadership ability. Personal qualities are important, and so are professional competencies that can be acquired in the classroom and on the field of play. A background in anatomy, biomechanics, communications, human relations, skill development, public relations, motor learning, physiology, psychology, sociology, and learning systems, as well as experience in the game itself, are important. The coach should have an understanding of man's social development, the physical and mental makeup of the individual, how one learns, and the place of the game in the education of the total man. Skills in meeting the needs of the individual, working effectively with participants, organizations, public relations, using resource materials efficiently and evaluating individual performances as well as team results should be developed and utilized. Many skills are needed because the coach assumes so many different roles—instructor, salesman, psychologist, parent, and business person.

The principles, guides to determine how the program will be set up, should be based upon both facts and philosophical judgement. Knowledge of facts can be gained through one's own experimentation or by reading or hearing the results of others' research. Old facts may not be absolute and new facts are being discovered so one should not become complacent with his current knowledge.

Philosophy

Philosophical judgement will be influenced by past experiences and personal philosophy. What has happened in the past (such as having been taught to win at any cost, been a benchwarmer instead of a star, been taught that defense is the key to winning, or having played on a closely knit team) affects one's present actions. The coach's personal philosophy is a dominating influence.

An idealist will set a good example. Individual differences will be considered and it will be important for each individual to develop to his full potential. The player will be given every chance to play. It is important that everyone be given an equal chance so it may take some time before the starting lineup is finalized. The player will be expected to play fair, obey the rules, and exhibit good sportsmanship. Even though great emphasis is placed upon the individual, teamwork is important. The idealist is interested in developing the whole person—personality, mind, character, citizenship, and behavior in general.

The realist will be systematic, firm, orderly, and logical in the presentation of materials. This coach will be more impersonal than the idealist and can be a disciplinarian as knowledge is dispensed. The development of fitness and skill are important and the players may be "run through" a very vigorous program. The lineup will be set at an early date and it may be very difficult to break up this group. The game plans will be adapted to the players—are they fast runners but weak hitters, slow runners but heavy hitters, strong offensively but weak defensivsly, strong defensively but weak offensively. Weak hitters will find themselves at the bottom of the batting order, those with little talent will sit on the bench, players with a good bat but weak arm will play someplace where the ball is not hit (if that is possible). The development of the individual is not really important except to improve team play.

The pragmatist's practice will be more informal than the realist's. Individuals are important and the reasons why something is being done will be explained to them. Players will be taught to think and reason. They will enjoy the practices, which will be useful, as well as playing the games. Players will be free to try new things and different positions. A lineup will be set and if this is successful, it will remain the same. If it doesn't work, something new will happen.

The existentialist will focus on the player as an individual. Players will have more freedom than with other types of philosophers but will have to accept responsibility for the consequences. They are there because they want to be—playing softball "just because." The quest for excellence, both for the individual and the team, is supported but one will strive in one's own way. There may be no goal or objectives for the team—each player chooses his own, the coach acts as a helper. Players may play several positions before finding one that will help contribute the team's success.

Many coaches have an eclectic philosophy—they blend parts from several philosophies making it difficult to classify them.

The role of the coach is a vital one, an essential part of a team. It would be relatively easy if all one had to do was teach the fundamentals but a coach is many things to many people. A tremendous responsibility is assumed when one chooses to be a coach.

Planning for the Year

Plan systematically. Begin by answering several questions. First, what is the goal for the year—to win the League Championship, win more games than last year, give players the basic fundamentals and look to the next year, instill a love for the game, or keep the players out of trouble?

Then, what are the needs of the players? Perhaps this should be the first question. Do they need to develop a good self-concept, learn the fundamentals, know the joy of being a part of a group, find something to keep them busy, or find success at something?

Next, what are the objectives? What should be accomplished quickly—develop a high level of physical fitness, improve the playing skills, develop acceptable social behavior, or show an interest in the game?

Are there other people involved—assistant coaches, maintenance personnel, business manager, athletic director? Will other teams be using the same facilities?

What program can be given to the players that will enable the goals and objectives to be met? Using the available facilities, personnel, and available equipment how can the program be designed to meet the needs of the team members and program.

How will the results be evaluated? Will there be input from the players as well as making use of the statistics that can be kept for the individual players and the team as a whole? What will be done with the evaluation? The season will be over but what about next year—can this information be fed back into the program and used to improve it?

After answering these questions relative to the specific situation, devise a scope and sequence chart or schedule to establish what must be dealt with during the year and in what order.

Preseason

Orientation

Plan a meeting with team members prior to the first scheduled practice. Outline the entire season—begin with the present time and take the players through the preparatory and competitive stages. The players should know what will be expected of them and what to expect from the program. A printed handout will help to eliminate possible problems.

State the goals and objectives for the year. The players have different ones for themselves, but they should be aware of what the coach has in mind. The coach should also be aware of what the players have as their goals. An information questionnaire should be completed by each player. Design one specific to the situation—ask for information that is useful. There may be one available that is used by the league or school.

Team Standards

Explain the team standards. Be explicit so that there is no misunderstanding. Keep them simple and realistic. Failure to comply should result in some type of disciplinary action. Coaches who set regulations should be fair and consistent in the treatment of those who fail to follow these requirements. Some coaches choose to talk with the players about

Scope and Sequence Chart

Activity	Preseason	Season	Postseason
Orientation			
Objectives and goals	x		
Player information	x		
Team standards	x		
Eligibility rules	x		
Safety procedures	x		
Practice schedule	x		
Competitive schedule	x		
Physical examination	x		
Locker room procedures	x		
Team finances	x		
Uniform assignments	x		
Multisport players	x		
Team selection	x		
Selection of a Manager	x		
Equipment	x		
Publicity	x		
Photographs	x		
Brochures	x		
Schedule cards	x		
Confirmation of Officials	x		
Preparation of Facilities	x		
Selection of a Captain	x		
Practice Sessions	x	x	
Conditioning Program	x	x	x
Basic Fundamentals	x	x	
Running	x		
Throwing			
Overhand	x		
Sidearm	x		
Underhand	x		
Catching	x		
Fielding			
Ground balls	x		
Fly balls	x		
Batting	x		
Offensive Play	x	x	
Place hitting	x		
Base running	x		

Activity	Preseason	Season	Postseason
Stealing	X		
Straight	X		
Delayed	X		
Single	X		
Double	X		
Hit and run	X		
Bunting			
Bunt and run	X		
Sacrifice			
Suicide	X		
Squeeze	X		
Safety	X		
Tagging up	X		
Coach's signals	X		
Defensive Play	X		
Position play			
Infield	X		
Outfield	X		
Pitcher	X		
Catcher	X		
Double play			
Runner on first	X		
Runner on second	X		
Runners on first and second	X		
Runners on first and third	X		
Fake and throw to third	X		
Bunting			
Sacrifice			
Runner on first	X		
Runner on second	X		
Runners on first and second	X		
Runners on first and third	X		
Squeeze	X		
Suicide	X		
Hit and run	X		
Stealing			
Double	X		
Single	X		
Rundown	X		
Backing up bases	X		
Special situations			
Team ahead	X		
Team behind	X		

Activity	Preseason	Season	Postseason
Scouting	x	x	
Statistics	x	x	
Coaching the game			
Pregame practice		x	
Lineup		x	
Use of the bench			
Home Games			
Field		x	
Officials		x	
Away Games			
Transportation		x	
Meals		x	
Housing		x	
Itinerary		x	
Evaluation			x
Scheduling			
Facilities			x
Officials			x
Games			x
Equipment	x		
Inventory			x
Repair/clean		x	x
Storage			x
Purchasing			x
Recruiting			x
Budget	x		x

common sense habits but do not establish specific regulations. Players are put on their own and, if common sense living habits are not observed, this shows up quickly when the players cannot do their work. Other coaches establish rules and include such items as:

1. Grooming—There is no specific length for the hair but it must be clean, pulled back out of the face when playing. Dress nicely when traveling—no jeans, shirt tails are to be tucked in, shoes will be shined, socks will be worn, and everything will be clean.
2. Sleeping—Be in bed by 11:00 on nights before games. Try to get at least eight hours sleep each night.
3. Eating—Eat sensibly and well. Do not overload with junk foods

_____ University

Softball Questionnaire

FULL NAME_____ PREFERRED NAME_____

SCHOOL ADDRESS _____ PHONE NUMBER _____

HOME ADDRESS _____ PHONE NUMBER _____

HEIGHT _____ WEIGHT _____ AGE _____ BIRTHDATE _____

MARRIED _____ SPOUSE'S NAME _____

CHILDREN'S NAMES _____

MAJOR ____ CLASSIFICATION ____ GRADUATION DATE ____

OVERALL GPA __ HOURS COMPLETED __ HOURS ENROLLED __

PROFESSIONAL OBJECTIVES _____

_____

YEARS OF ELIGIBILITY REMAINING (including present one) _____

SOFTBALL OBJECTIVES _____

_____

PREVIOUS SOFTBALL EXPERIENCE _____

_____

COLLEGES AND UNIVERSITIES ATTENDED _____

_____

ATHLETIC ACHIEVEMENTS _____

_____

BIGGEST THRILL IN SPORTS _____

_____

WHY ARE YOU PLAYING SOFTBALL _____

_____

WHY DID YOU CHOOSE THIS SCHOOL _____

_____

such as candy bars, potato chips, carbonated beverages, or items loaded with carbohydrates.
4. Smoking—Do not smoke during the playing season.
5. Attending Classes—Do not miss class.
6. Responsibility—You are responsible for the uniforms assigned to you. Keep then clean, in good repair, and return the week after the season ends.
7. Drugs—Avoid at all times.

Eligibility Rules

The coach must be fully aware of all eligibility rules of national, state, league, and/or school agencies. Time should be taken to thoroughly explain these to the participants. There can be several factors involved—the number of years of participation, transfer regulations, grade point average, courses completed or passed, what constitutes a full-time student, what is considered professionalism, scholarship regulations. Make it a point to check on each player. Taking a player's word may be an unwise decision as they may not be aware of all regulations.

Practice Regulations

Establish practice regulations before the sessions get underway. As with the other regulations, explain these in great detail so that there is no misunderstanding. Typical information would include:

1. Practice sessions will be held Monday-Friday on fields one and two from 3:15 until 5:15.
2. Be on time. If you expect to be late or unable to attend, inform the coach prior to the session.
3. Wear clean clothing. This is a healthful practice as well as an indication of personal pride.
4. Wear suitable and comfortable clothing to permit you to move freely and safely. Wear a warm-up suit if you choose but you must wear one if the temperature drops below 50°.
5. Wear softball (soccer or field hockey) shoes that are in good repair. This is a safety factor as well as allowing you to move more efficiently.
6. Take care of the equipment. If you check it out, return it. Keep the equipment on the field in the assigned areas.
7. Follow safety precautions.
   a. Keep your nails clipped.
   b. Leave your jewelry at home or in the locker room.
   c. Do not leave equipment strewn on the field.

d.　Stretch and loosen up thoroughly at the beginning of each practice.

e.　Be aware of what is happening on the field at all times.

f.　Report all injuries and illnesses.

8.　Shower and change clothes at the end of each session.

Competitive Schedule

When discussing the schedule include times, dates, days, and places in the information. Give the total schedule. This should have been set in the previous year and there should be few changes. The players can make arrangements concerning classes, work, and/or family when they know the full schedule in advance.

Physical Examinations

Do not send the players through a workout until after they have had a thorough physical examination. This policy or rule is stated in the handbooks of many conferences and leagues. If at all possible, make sure that the examination is a complete one and includes a tentanus shot. The coach should read the completed reports very carefully and then place them in the players' files.

Locker Room Procedures

There may be a special locker room for the athletes and if not, perhaps they could have a special corner of the regular locker room. Long lockers are need for storing equipment and uniforms. Towels should be available after each practice session and game. If there is a fee, the players should be made aware of the cost.

Finances

The budget is set early in the current year or late in the previous year so there should be no reason for the coach to misunderstand the situation. In turn, the coach may be wise to explain the financial situation to the players. A view of the total picture can be very educational. They need to know what expenses will be paid—meals, travel, housing. If they are expected to help finance their endeavors, inform them before the season begins.

Uniforms

Inform the team members as to what uniforms and special equipment will be available. If there are uniforms, when will they be checked out, where, and by whom. Give specific instructions regarding care of garments and consequences if a piece is lost or ruined. Are the players expected to furnish their own shoes and gloves? Establish a return date. Leave nothing to speculation.

Team Selection

Make this process as objective as possible. Inform the players of the cutting date(s), the criteria to be used, and the number of players that will remain with the team. If there are some players, example scholarship recipients or returning players, who will be kept on the squad, this should also be included in the information.

The individual situation will determine many policies. If a team has six weeks of preseason practice and a large number of players trying for a place, there may be a cut at the end of the first two weeks and a final cut after the first four. Fourteen or fifteen may be a workable number for a game but will not supply enough personnel for an intra-squad practice game. There is always the possibility that injuries or illnesses will deplete a squad. The number of available uniforms may make the decision regarding the number of players to remain. "Do not cut anyone" is the philosophy of many coaches but there are situations in which there are not enough coaches, space, equipment, or money to handle an unlimited number.

The criteria should be based upon the abilities needed to play the game. Speed is essential, a fast movement time is helpful, a good aim is a must, fielding is important, and hitting is vital. Items that can be measured either in drills or in a game include:

1. Speed.
   a. Running from home to first.
   b. Running from home to second.
   c. Running from first to second.
2. Distance and/or velocity of an overhand throw.
3. Time needed to react to a visual signal and take two steps.
4. Offensive percentages (based upon a minimum of nine times at bat).
   a. Hits.
   b. Total bases.
   c. Runs batted in.
5. Defensive percentages (based upon play in a minimum of three practice games).
   a. Fielding.
   b. Throwing.

Being skillful is not the only thing to consider. Drive and desire to play offset a skill weakness. A spirit of cooperation and team play, self-discipline, and a desire to excel are very important. One irritable, selfish player can destroy a team's solidarity, so good personal qualities are important traits to consider in selecting team members.

Injuries
The coach and/or the trainer should discuss good health habits, personal hygiene, and injury treatment. Though the coach is not a doctor or a nurse and should not assume these roles, it is the coach's responsibility to see that all injuries are recognized and given proper treatment. Players should be encouraged to report such conditions as abrasions, athletes foot, blisters, contusions, and pulled muscles as well as illnesses. Inform them that first aid equipment will be available at all practices and games and is to be used but not abused.

Multi-Sport Participation
Whether or not a player can participate in more than one sport in a season or in the year is a decision that more and more coaches and/or program administrators are having to make. Many players are all-round athletes and conflicts between sports are inevitable. The individual's health and academic standing should be the primary concerns, not the need of the team or the school. It is very difficult, both mentally and physically, for a player to take part in two programs at the same time or even to move directly from one sport to another. There may need to be a recuperative period. If the program has no policy, the decision is left to the individual coach who should inform the players of his decisions. The involved players should have an opportunity to discuss this with the coach.

Selection of a Manager

A nonplaying manager is a must. The coach has to perform innumerable tasks and many of these can be assigned to a good manager. This is an important job so the selection should be made very carefully. Select one who is capable and willing to work. Post the duties before making the selection to give the applicants an opportunity to be familiar with the expectations because some may wish to withdraw their applications. The duties are many and varied and some authority will need to be given with the responsibility. A manager may be expected to:

1. Equipment:
   a. Keep an up-to-date inventory.
   b. Keep a record of the equipment issued.
   c. Clean and repair equipment.
   d. Check for faulty equipment.
   e. Keep a record of what is being used.

2. On the field
    a. Have equipment on the field prior to practices and games.
    b. Keep a fresh supply of water.
    c. Check the field for proper preparation.
    d. Help prepare the field.
    e. Remove loose and unnecessary equipment from the area.
    f. Keep notes and statistics.
    g. Return equipment at the end of the practice or game.
3. On the road
    a. Post a list of the personnel making the trip.
    b. Pack equipment and place it on the bus.
    c. Have a bag to be used to keep players' valuables.
    d. Get water for the bench.
    e. Arrange equipment.
    f. Obtain towels for use during and after the game.
    g. Check equipment for the return trip.
    h. Unload equipment and return it to the equipment room.

Publicity

Attempt to place the team before the student body and/or community. Publicity angles should be sought to promote the team. Information about individual players and team plans should be given to school and community papers, radio and television stations, and placed in display areas. Make arrangements for media representatives to come to the practices to meet the players and get a first hand look at the team. Have pictures available for use by television stations and newspapers. The coach should take advantage of every opportunity to meet and speak to various groups on campus or in the community. In a school cooperate with other departments—art, journalism, communications, speech—that may be eager to give invaluable assistance. Often a business establishment will support a team by having billfold size schedules printed. Do not hesitate to seek favorable publicity to build a favorable image of the team.

Confirmation of Officials

Contracts should have been made and signed during the post-season phase of the previous year. For this year's play, copies of these transactions should be on file. All that is necessary now is to check with each official to confirm the time, day, date, place, and fee. A form letter can be sent on each official or contact may be made by telephone. Many things can happen between seasons and reminding the officials of their obligations will help prevent unnecessary problems.

Equipment Check

The season should not begin without a check of the equipment. All items should have been cleaned, repaired, and stored at the end of the previous season. New equipment should have been received, checked off, marked, and made ready for immediate use. However, to assume that everything is ready for the season can be a mistake. The inventory should be rechecked to make sure that the equipment is there. If some item is needed or something has to be repaired, there is time to do it before play begins.

Preparing Facilities

Hopefully, this maintenance duty will be the responsibility of someone other than the coach. If it is, the coach is still ultimately responsible for making sure the responsibility is fulfilled. A list of what has to be done and the time it is to be done should be made and posted. Check the fences and backstop for holes, smooth and rake the infield, check the outfield for holes, align the bases and foul lines, paint the dugout, get new numbers for the scoreboard, replace bleacher boards, and check the concession stand. If a complete checklist is made, it will make the job much easier.

Selecting a Captain

The coach may choose to appoint a captain at the beginning of the season or one for each game in order to have one that is capable and to avoid petty politics and popularity contests. If this is done, the team may select an honorary captain at the end of the season. However it is done, the selection should be made with great care. Responsibility accompanies this position and if the captain is selected by the team, the responsibilities should be specified in advance. A captain turns in lineups for games, clarifies rules, handles discussions with the umpires, acts as an intermediary between the players and the coach, helps with the practices, represents the team and coach on and off the field, and is a pacifier of complaints.

Practice Sessions

Plan each practice carefully. These are conditioning sessions as well as technical and tactical ones. Every possible play situation must be covered before the season begins. Be prepared to demonstrate and explain correct actions and teach the players to think in correct patterns. Avoid overly long tedious drills and practice sessions and be flexible enough to adjust workouts to the team's progress.

The amount of emphasis given to the three areas—conditioning, technique, and strategy, will depend upon the length of the preseason. If it is to be two months in length, the work in the first month would be divided into fifty percent conditioning, forty percent technique, and ten percent strategy. The emphasis would then shift away from conditioning—thirty percent during the second month to forty percent technique and thirty percent strategy. The three areas should not be dealt with independently but dealt with concurrently. Teach the physiological and biomechanical principles, the why along with the how, for exercises and drills. Players should be aware of the relationship between these concepts and successful game play.

A daily practice schedule may be broken down into:

1. Warm-up and stretching exercises.
2. Technique drills.
3. Team drills.
4. Sprints.

A further breakdown would be: (minutes)

1. Loosen up by playing catch and pepper (15)
2. Group exercises (10)
   stretching
   jogging
3. Fundamental drills (15)
   infield practice fielding ground balls
   outfield practice fielding fly balls and ground balls
4. Batting practice (60)
   Infielders are fielding these hits and fungoes
   Outfielders are fielding these hits and fungoes
5. Infield drill—pregame routine (10)
6. Infield-outfield drills (15)
7. Sprints (10)

Scouting

Take a look at the opposing team's offense to find out about the:

1. Hitting—Who pulls the ball, hits to the opposite field, has power, place hits, hits through the middle?
2. Batting—What pitches do they like to hit? Are they first ball hitters? Do they crowd the plate, stand deep or shallow, step back from the base?

3. Baserunners—Who is fast, likely to try for extra bases, challenges the fielder?
4. Team—Does it go for the big innings? Is it a running team, a power team, or both? Do the players steal, bunt, hit, and run?

The play of the defense is equally important. Look at the:

1. Pitcher—Does he have a set pattern, any habits? What happens when he is behind the hitter? Is he afraid of balls being hit through the middle? Is the first pitch usually a strike? How does he react with runners on base?
2. Catcher—Can he catch and throw? Is he afraid to block the plate?
3. Infielders—Are they fast? Can they throw, defense against bunts, move to the right and left? Do they play deep or shallow?
4. Outfielders—Are they fast? Do they have strong arms, difficulty in working together? Do they play deep or shallow, hesitate before throwing the ball? In slow pitch is the fourth fielder, an infielder or an outfielder.

Statistics

Statistics have many uses—to select members of the team, find individual strengths and weaknesses, determine the amount of time that should be spent on certain aspects of the game, give feedback to the players, indicate the importance of each aspect of the game, serve as a basis for individual awards, and to provide information for the news media.

Basic computations for offensive efficiency include:

1. Batting Average—Total number of hits divided by the official times at bat.
2. Runs Batted In Percentage—Total number of runs batted in divided by composite total of walks, total hits, number of times hit by the pitcher.
3. On Base Percentage—Composite total of number of walks, times hit by the pitcher, and hits divided by the composite total of walks, times hit by the pitcher, and total times at bat.
4. Slugging Percentage—Total number of bases divided by the number of official times at bat.
5. Stolen Base Percentage—The number of stolen bases divided by the composite total of number of hits, walks, times hit by the pitcher.
6. Sacrifice Percentage—Total number of sacrifices divided by the composite total of sacrifices and official times at bat.

7. Runs Percentage—Total number of runs divided by the composite total of walks, times hit by the pitcher, and total hits.
8. Strikeout Percentage—Number of strikeouts divided by the total number of official times at bat.
9. Walk Percentage—Total number of walks divided by the composite total of walks and official trips to the plate.

Usually there are not as many statistics kept on defensive play as on offensive play. Basic computations for defensive efficiency include:

1. Fielding Percentage—Total number errors divided by the total number of fielding chances. (This can be broken down into errors made when fielding a batted ball, errors made on throws, and errors made when catching a thrown ball.)
2. Pitching Efficiency (strikeout percentage)—Total number of strikeouts divided by total number of batters faced.
3. Pitching Efficiency (hitting percentage)—Total number of hits divided by the total number of innings pitched or by the number of games pitched.
4. Pitching Efficiency (earned runs percentage)—The total number of earned runs scored (exclusive of runs scored as a result of fielding errors) divided by the total number of innings pitched or by the number of games pitched.

Coaching the Game

On the day before the game have a light practice. The pitcher should work easily; batting practice should be in the form of a game. The team should go through the game day warm-up drill, practice relays and cut-offs, run, and then discuss the plans for the next day. Players should not get tired but keep loose and prepare mentally and physically for the coming game.

On the day of the game the players should dress and be ready for a team meeting about two hours before game time. Those players who need to be taped or receive any special attention from the trainer should report earlier. A typical schedule would be:

1:40 Meet in the locker room, announce lineup, go over game plan.
1:55 Take the field together and warm-up.
2:00 Batting practice.
2:30 Opponent's batting practice (watch for half the time before playing catch and pepper).
3:00 Opponent's take infield.
3:12 Infield practice.

3:25 Off the field (copy of ground rules and lineup to umpire and opponents).
3:30 Game begins.

Before pregame practice begins take a look at the field. If it is wet, bunts can be used more effectively, baserunners must begin their slides sooner, and outfielders should charge ground balls. If the field is sunny, have glasses or caps for the players and inform them to be ready to help each other keep track of the ball. The wind will affect the flight of the fly ball or slowly pitched ball. Note the direction and whether or not it is gusting or blowing steadily.

Game Day Practice Drills

Have the entire team take the field to go through the drills quickly and efficiently. This can be used as a psychological factor by lifting team spirits as well as impressing the opponents. A typical drill series would be:

1. Outfield round (field fungo ground balls)
   a. Ball is thrown to second base
      Hit to leftfielder's right
      Hit to centerfielder's right
      Hit to rightfielder's left
   b. Ball is thrown to third base
      Hit directly to the fielders
   c. Ball is thrown home
      Hit directly to the fielders but well in front
2. Outfielders move to deep center to field fungo balls
3. Infield round (field fungo ground balls)
   a. Catcher throws to each position
   b. Hit directly to each position
      Fielder throws to first base
      First throws to catcher
      Catcher throws to fielder (at the base) who started the play
      That fielder throws to third who throws to the catcher
      Ball hit to first, throw goes to second base
      Ball rolled toward third for catcher
   c. Hit ball to left of each infielder
      Fielder throws to first base
      Ball is thrown around in the same pattern as b
      Ball is rolled toward the pitcher for the catcher
   d. Double play
      Hit ball to the left of third and shortstop who throws to second

Hit ball to right of second and first who throws to second
Fielder covering second throws to first who throws to catcher
Ball is thrown around as in b
Ball rolled toward first for the catcher

e.   Double play
Same as d except ball is dropped in front of the plate for the catcher and the balls are hit in the opposite direction to each player

f.   Hit ball to right of each position
Fielder throws ball to first
First throws to third who throws back to first who throws home
Catcher throws ball to third after fielding a roller

g.   Hit slow roller to each
Fielder throws to first who throws home
First throws the roller home

h.   Hit a slow roller to each
Fielder throws home

i.   Hit a pop fly to each
Throw comes home and fielders follow

The Bench

Everyone on the team should be in the game, mentally and spiritually if not physically. All players should get to play in the game if possible so that all have "their chance," but this is an individual coach's decision. Some coaches set a lineup and use substitutes sparingly, while others make sure that everyone plays, especially if the team is playing a doubleheader. The players on the bench should focus their attention on the game. Not only can they give vocal encouragement that contributes to the morale of those on the field but they can uncover valuable information by studying the opposing team.

They should be ready to come into the game as a pinchhitter, pinch runner, or defensive specialist. A pinchhitter may be used to: hit the long ball (a long fly ball can score a run), bunt (fast and can get on base or sacrifice to move a runner into scoring position), place hit (avoid a double play or hit behind the runner), or get a hit (a good clutch hitter). A pinch runner is often used to replace a slow runner on the base paths; speed is essential. Oftentimes, usually in the late innings when a team is ahead by a limited number of runs, a good defensive player is sent in. His "bat" is not needed but his defensive skills are. Remember, however, any player removed from the game cannot return.

Many coaches use substitutes as base coaches. This may occur if there are not assistant coaches and the coach prefers to remain on the bench to watch the game as a whole or simply to allow fuller participation for those team members. Knowledgeable players should be used; they cannot be hesitant in making quick decisions. They must also be capable of carrying out the coach's decisions.

Home Games

The coach is the one responsible for making sure the field is ready and that the officials know the correct date, time, and place. These duties may be assigned to assistants, but the coach is ultimately responsible. A phone call the night before may prevent an unnecessary delay of the game and embarrassment, as well as the development of poor public relations.

Away Games

School policy or community custom will set transportation guidelines. Plans should be formulated when the schedule is set the previous year. Whatever the policies may be, the coach should be aware of them and pass the information to the players. Determine the mode of transportation (school or commercial bus, private cars, school cars, rental cars) and the drivers (parents, students, faculty members, bus driver) and make reservations well in advance. Make sure that there is good insurance coverage, especially if private cars are being used. This can be a dangerous practice even though the car and driver may be well insured. Some team sponsors use a van or recreational vehicle to transport the team.

Itinerary

In many instances it is required, and at all times it is a good idea, to prepare an itinerary. Information should be included as to when the team will leave, the departure point, where the team is going, where it will stay, the playing schedule, and the time and date of return. Players, school personnel, parents, and others should have this information well in advance. It would also be helpful for the players to know what to pack other than their playing gear. Is a towel needed, will there be a dinner that requires "dressy" clothes, would a blanket and pillow come in handy on the bus? Will money be needed for meals?

Plan the trip well. An alternative plan should be made—a driver may become ill, the bus can break down, a road can close, or the weather may get bad. Know how to get where you are going; the bus driver should know but the area may be new to him. Prior arrangements should be made with the home team in regard to dressing rooms, lockers, towels, and shower facilities. Arrange for expense money for meals and emergencies—a player may be injured or become ill, there may be an accident, or someone may get lost. Plan to leave in plenty of time to be at the field at least two hours before the game is scheduled.

If it will be an overnight or extended trip, the itinerary should include practice times, free times, meal times, in-room times, rest times, and bed times. Time should not hang heavy nor should the players be permitted to roam free to get tired and/or lost. Plans may be made for sightseeing or shopping. The coach has to be the judge in determining whether or not the players need to be supervised closely or whether they can be left on their own.

A strict coach may choose to give an information sheet to the players. This sheet could include such information as:

1. The purpose of this trip is to play softball. All personnel will travel together, eat together, stay together unless permission is secured from the coach prior to the trip.
2. Dress neatly and in good taste. The coach reserves the right to be the judge.
3. Please note the times of departure and return. You may not make the trip if you are not ready at departure time, and you may not make another trip if you are not ready at return time.
4. Pack what you need and only what you need. You are responsible for your uniform and equipment.
5. Remember you are representing yourself, the team and/or the school and community. Smoking, drinking alcoholic beverages, cursing, using drugs, using obscenties, and being loud and boisterous will not be tolerated.
6. Watch what you eat. Do not overeat or eat rich foods that do not agree with you. The best guide is to eat what you eat at home.
7. There will be no rest stops while enroute to and from the game. Do not cram yourself with cold drinks, candy, and potato chips along the way. This rule will be relaxed on the return trip but do not make yourself ill.
8. Observe price limitations for the meals—$5.50 for dinner, $2.50 for lunch, and $2.00 for breakfast. If you order above this limit, you pay the difference. The coach will pay for the meals; no money will be given to the player.
9. Two of you will be assigned to each room. Roommates will not be assigned unless your actions make it necessary. Observe these assignments and be in your room by 9:30 and in bed by 10:30.

10. At the motel do not make phone calls, use room service, or request any services from your room unless you pay for these as soon as the requests are fulfilled.
11. At no time take any souvenirs that have not been paid for. This includes such items as towels, ash trays, silverware, salt and pepper shakers.
12. You are responsible for your actions even though you have the support of the team, coach, and school.

Post-Season

Evaluation

The coach should talk with the players throughout the season but particularly at the end of the season to get their final evaluation. Some may choose to give a questionnaire to complete while others may elect to have a final meeting for this purpose. Regardless of the choice of methods, it is important for the coach to know the view of the year from the standpoint of the participants as their observations should help to plan for the next year. And if the players do not volunteer information, the coach should ask questions. Ask what was good and bad, was the emphasis on the right areas, were the drills too long, were the practices useful—anything to give a lead to the players.

An anonymous questionnaire might be a better idea as the players may feel more free to express themselves. One should be made that can be answered objectively and contain questions that have a direct bearing on the team.

The coach should take a good long look at the past season, not only at the won-loss record but at the team accomplishment of objectives that were set at the beginning of the season. If these were not reached, what should be done? Were the goals realistic, was the season poorly planned, was the execution wrong, were the personnel too authoritarian? Be objective in the evaluation. The findings should be used in planning for the coming year.

Scheduling

Making a schedule is a difficult task. Oftentimes the school or league devises it, but the coach usually has the final word. Complete the schedule as soon as possible and consider such things as:

1. The effect on the players' academic standing and/or work schedule.

2. The amount of money in the budget.
3. The inexperienced team needs victories at the beginning.
4. The games with arch rivals should be played after a rest or easy game.
5. The short "first class" trips may be better than long second or third class ones.
6. A long trip should include more than one game.
7. A team should have an even chance for a victory in seventy-five percent of its games.
8. A long road trip should end with a Saturday game to give some rest before Monday.
9. The away games may be less expensive than the home games.
10. The schedule should include enough games to ensure a good competitive season if there is a lot of rain, but not overwork a team if it is a dry season and all games are played.
11. The scheduling for the team should be coordinated with other school or community activities.

Officials

It is a good idea to rate officials during the season. If one does not perform satisfactorily, plan not to use him for future games. If they are paid mileage and per deim allowances as well as a flat rate for the game, look for competent officials near at hand. Have contracts prepared for them to sign. This obligates the umpire and the school or league and is a good business practice. If officials are not signed until just before the playing season begins, the coach may have to settle for ones less capable.

Facilities

Do not schedule games unless the facilities are available. Get the dates and times for practices and games on the school and community calendars. Make sure that facilities are reserved for the team. Again, this should not be done at the last minute but in the post-season part of the previous year. Waiting until preseason to reserve facilities may turn the season into a disaster.

Equipment

Every item that has been checked out should be returned immediately at the end of the competitive season. The manager should take an inventory, checking against the list that was used at the beginning of the year, check for faulty equipment, and have repairs made before placing anything in storage. A list should be made of items to be purchased and an order should be placed immediately. A list should be kept throughout the year so that everything that is needed will be ordered. It takes time to complete an order so this should be done well ahead of the preseason. The purchase list should be correlated with an up-to-date inventory that gives number of items on hand, their condition, when they were purchased, from whom, the cost, and the sizes.

Budget

It is difficult to plan a program if there is no budget or if the budget is not known. Be realistic in planning one but be sure that all necessary aspects of the program are funded. A budget request may be submitted, or the coach may be told that a set amount of money is available and plans should be based upon this. However the budget is to be established, do this during the post-season. Base the projected budget on the current year's expenses, the need for replenishing supplies and equipment, planned expansions, and then add ten percent for inflation. Present an itemized list to the proper authority including items such as equipment, uniforms, officials, facilities, travel, lodging, meals, phone calls, postage, medical expenses, awards, insurance, and publicity.

If the coach is unsure of needs and/or cost, it is helpful to seek advice from someone who has had experience in this area. Copies of all transactions should be kept on file. Orders placed by phone should be followed immediately by a written copy. Complete records must be kept. Ask the financial office for statements several times during the year and compare these with records kept in the office. It is a good business practice to know the current amount of money in the budget as this can help avoid financial problems.

Recruiting

Keep recruiting legal and ethical. There are rules that regulate the actions of the coach, some written and others unwritten. A coach is responsible for knowing what is legal and should do nothing to jeopardize the player, team, or school. After the season has been evaluated, the coach should know the needs of the team for the next year. Perhaps the pitcher graduated and new ones must be found, the team lacked speed and a long ball hitter, or there is a need for a utility infielder. There should be a systematic plan for recruiting players; otherwise, one may end with a very unbalanced team, unhappy players, financial troubles, and ultimately a poor season. The players should be seen in action before they are actively recruited, but this is not always possible. At times it will be necessary to rely on another coach's evaluation, the player's statistics, or a friend's scouting report. The need of the individual being recruited should be the primary concern of the coach; the need of the team is secondary. A coach should not promise more than can be given and must remember that the recruit is first a person, then a student (if it is a school team), and then a softball player.

Chapter 13

Teaching

Teaching is different from coaching, although good teachers and good coaches share the same qualities of knowledge, skill, understanding, and concern for the player. The teacher deals with a variety of skill levels and interests and has a different goal that places learning above winning. Although the content is the same, the teacher must measure student progress by accomplishment of stated objectives while the coach often measures success through game statistics.

Planning for teaching depends on several factors; purposes of instruction, teacher interest, teacher philosophy, student characteristics, class schedule, school policies, and the place of softball in the total curriculum. There are serious questions that must be answered before teaching plans can be completed. These are discussed in this chapter.

Preliminary Considerations for Planning

The entire softball instructional program rests on the teacher's and/or faculty's perception of what is to be accomplished. The aims (long range) and objectives (short range) must be determined. Other questions must also be answered. Will the students be asked to establish objectives for themselves? Will the students have to throw accurately and/or for distance, hit the ball out of the infield, run fast, know the rules in minute detail? Should they develop minimal skills to allow them to play for "fun" or are they to be readied for varsity play at a later date?

The teacher must determine the place of softball in his value structure, as well as its place in the physical education hierarchy. Do you, the teacher, like the game? Is it one of your favorites or are you teaching this because no one else will? Are you highly skilled or are you one that played right field because few balls are hit to that area? If fast pitch is your game, should you choose to teach it even if everyone in your locale plays slow pitch? Are you a pragmatist and believe that a class should be useful or an idealist who thinks that moral values and sportsmanship should play a very important part?

What is the place of the course in the physical education hierarchy? Is this the only softball unit taught is grades 6-12? Is this to be the basic skills course because the playing strategies will be stressed in the other grades?

Knowledge of student characteristics is a priority for planning all instruction. The students must not be forgotten; in fact they should be the first consideration. What are their age levels, skill levels, interests, developmental characteristics? Are they choosing to play the game or is this another requirement? Have they played before? Will there be an opportunity to play outside of class?

The teacher/planner must have specific information about facilities and equipment. Where will the game be played? What are the available facilities? Does the diamond have a paved, sand, grass, or clay surface? What is the size of the playing area; how many diamonds can be laid out? What equipment is available? All teachers need to take into account administrative considerations of schedule, attendance, dress, and grading.

Will the class meet every day, every other day, twice a week? How long are the class periods—fifty minutes, thirty minutes, twice a week for seventy-five minutes, or three times for twenty-five minutes? How many weeks will be spent in teaching the game; will it be time-based or competency-based? What do the students wear for play? May they dress as they choose or must they wear something suitable for playing? Will they miss class each week to sing, march, or drive? Perhaps they meet in class every other day as they alternate with another course or else they come to class two weeks late. How many will be assigned to the class; what is the grading system; will the class be team taught? Is this class to be males, females, co-ed?

Ideal answers to these questions cannot be made to suit every situation. However, all teachers can hope for a softball unit that is valued by faculty and students, for softball diamonds prepared according to ASA standards, for sufficient equipment for each student to be properly and safely equipped, for small enough classes for good and safe instruction, and for students dressed safely and appropriately.

Organizing Instruction

When the foregoing preliminary considerations are determined for a particular school situation, instructional organization can begin. The sequencing of instruction in a systematic manner is necessary to ensure that all necessary skills, knowledges, and appreciations are involved.

One plan and style for organizing instructional materials can be found in C.O.P.E. (Curriculum Objectives of Physical Education).[1] The materials that follow are modeled after that plan and style.

There are five major areas to be included in the softball instructional package. These are: (1) introduction, (2) individual skills, (3) offense, (4) defense, and (5) evaluation. The scope and sequence chart presented here lists the recommended areas of instruction, the domain for which objectives should be written, and the levels to which instruction can be geared.

Preparing Objectives

New educational methods and the current stress on accountability requires the preparation of performance objectives that state explicit outcomes. Objectives in all domains—cognitive, psychomotor, and affective—can be prepared for the items listed on the scope and sequence chart. Criteria for performance can be established at the selected levels— beginner, intermediate, or advanced. Samples of performance objectives follow:

Affective Objectives

The student will demonstrate a concern for the welfare of other players by:

1. Throwing the ball with a force commensurate with the receiver's ability to catch.
2. Avoiding contact with a baseman when running or sliding into a base.
3. Refraining from hitting the ball into an area reserved for other skill drills.
4. Being certain the receiver is aware of an oncoming throw.

The student will demonstrate his interest in and appreciation of softball by:

1. Voicing satisfaction. ("I like this game.")
2. Stating enjoyment. ("This is fun.")
3. Practicing skills outside of class.
4. Playing on an intramural team.

---

1. Florida Department of Education, Tallahassee, Florida, 1975. Barb Landers and Janet Wells, Project Directors.

Item	Related Educational Objective Areas			Performance Criteria		
	Cognitive	Psychomotor	Affective	Beg	Inter	Adv
I. Introduction						
A. History	X			X		
B. Games	X			X		
C. Equipment	X		X	X	X	X
D. Rules	X			X	X	X
E. Safety	X		X	X		
F. Conditioning	X			X	X	X
II. Fundamental Skills						
A. Catching	X	X		X		
B. Throwing						
1. Overhand	X	X		X	X	X
2. Sidearm	X	X		X	X	X
C. Fielding						
1. Ground balls	X	X		X	X	X
2. Fly balls	X	X		X	X	X
D. Batting						
1. Basic	X	X		X		
2. Place hitting	X	X		X	X	
3. Bunting	X	X			X	X
E. Base Running						
1. To first base	X	X		X		
2. Extra bases	X	X		X		
3. Sliding	X	X			X	X
4. Stealing	X	X		X		
III. Offense						
A. Batting Order	X	X		X		
B. Hit and Run	X	X			X	X
C. Squeeze Play	X	X			X	X
D. Coaches	X	X		X		
E. Rules	X			X	X	X
IV. Defense						
A. Infield	X	X		X	X	
B. Pitching	X	X		X	X	X
C. Outfield	X	X		X	X	
D. Combined Defense	X	X		X	X	X
E. Situations						
1. Tagging runners	X	X				
2. Run down	X	X				
3. Team ahead	X	X				
4. Team behind	X	X				
F. Rules	X			X	X	X
V. Evaluation						
A. Cognitive						
1. Written exams	X			X	X	X
2. Playing the game	X			X	X	X
B. Psychomotor						
1. Skills tests		X		X	X	X
2. Playing the game		X		X	X	X
C. Affective			X	X	X	X

Cognitive Objectives

The student will demonstrate a knowledge of terminology by defining terms to standard.

Define the following: (see the current rule book for content)

1. Assist
2. Double Play
3. Error
4. Fielder's Choice
5. Foul Tip

Standard: Define all without error.

The student will demonstrate a knowledge of the use of equipment by listing two guidelines for purchasing a:

1. Glove
2. Bat
3. Shoes
4. Socks

Standard: List two for each piece without error.

Psychomotor Objectives

The student will demonstrate the ability to throw overhand correctly and accurately at a two-foot square target using style described in the text.

Beginner: 60 feet and hit the target 7 of 10 times.
Intermediate: 75 feet and hit the target 7 of 10 times.
Advanced: 90 feet and hit the target 7 of 10 times.

The student will demonstrate the ability to field a ground ball, without error, a ball hit from 60 feet away.

Beginner: At moderate speed and in a direct line 6 of 10 times.
Intermediate: At varying (slow, moderate, fast) speeds and to an area to the left or right 6 of 10 times.
Advanced: At varying speeds (slow, moderate, fast) speeds to the left or right 8 of 10 times.

Class Organization

There are special considerations for class organization including safety, class membership and grouping, use of student assistants, and use of teaching aids.

The safety of the students must be the primary concern. The teacher must be alert to safe instructional situations not only to ensure the welfare of the students but also to avoid the possibility of being held liable for student injury.

Stress safety procedures at all times. Post the safety rules in addition to discussing them at the beginning of the unit and possibly showing a film that demonstrates safety practices in a game. The playing area should be free of hazards and the proper equipment should be in good repair. Require the catchers to wear a mask and chest protector. Specify what is to be done in class, when, and where. If the group is warming-up by throwing, have the throws going in the same direction; make sure that there is room to execute the drill. Do not permit drill activity of one group to infringe on the space of another group.

Title IX permits classes organized in ability groups as well as co-educational classes that may have mixed skill levels. For co-ed classes, it might be wise to have the males bat from their nondominant side and/or use a sixteen inch or soft softball until skills are more equalized. Classes can also be organized in other ways—by grade groups, age groups, and on a selective or elective basis. Ability grouping can be determined by skills tests such as the AAHPER Softball skills tests or other tests devised by the teacher. This kind of grouping can be a safety factor in many instances and can avoid injury caused by mixing unskilled and skilled players.

Use the students as assistants but not as substitute teachers. They can help lay out the field—it could be a math assignment. Give each an opportunity to take the equipment out and bring it in. Post an assignment sheet so that all may know their duties ahead of time. Many are capable of giving corrective assistance to members of their peer group or at least being demonstrators for skills. Peer or reciprocal teaching can be effective and can enhance evaluation.

Technique charts and videotapes made of other student players can be used as teaching aids. Videotape the students in action and play it back for instant feedback. Give corrective assistance and use positive feedback, "praise," whenever possible during instruction. Films can be obtained from several different companies. Use equipment when explaining and if you cannot demonstrate the skill, have someone perform it who is highly skilled while an explanation is being given. Bring in a consultant or guest speaker from within the school or community for a lecture demonstration.

Give the students an opportunity to learn in different ways. Make a reading assignment in the library; utilize crossword puzzles (many can design their own) for learning definitions and rules. Provide opportunities for the "writer" to create, the artist to design, the historian to look back, and the mathematician to figure percentages. All are not highly skilled or are they equally interested in playing the game; however, there are different ways to learn about and be a part of the game.

Lead-up Games

Students would rather play than drill. Drills are means to develop the skills necessary to play but, as a motivational factor, get the students into some type of game early in the unit. Oftentimes a lead-up game will satisfy the desire to play as well as serving as a type of drill. The games should be as much like a softball game as possible in the number of players, skills used, field of play, and rules. Do not use a game or drill that violates standards of good play.

Scrub

The players select any of the nine or ten defensive positions while four or five become the batters. Official rules are used except there are no teams—the batter is generally on his own. If he makes an out, he moves to the defensive team outfield. In slow pitch lt would be position 10 (shortfielder), to work his way from 10 to 9 to 8 to 7 etc., until he is at bat again. If the batter hits a fly ball, he may switch places with the fielder who made the catch.

One-Pitch Softball

The hitting team provides the pitcher who cannot field the ball or interfere in anyway with the defense. The pitcher does not miss his turn at bat as another member of the batting team takes his place. Pitchers can be changed at any time. Each batter receives one pitch. He must hit a fair ball or he is out. Anything other than hitting the ball fair constitutes an out. He must take a full swing.

A baserunner cannot steal or slide. Members of the hitting team, other than those actively involved in the game plus the "on deck" batter, must be on the bench.

Fungo

The rules for the game, either slow pitch or fast pitch, are the same as for an official game except there is no pitching involved. The batter fungoes. Rules can be established to determine the outs—swing and miss, hit a foul ball, or the outfield when the ball is supposed to be handled by an infielder.

Five Person

Five players make a team. Five begin in the outfield (to make five positions add the shortstop to the four outfield ones), five others in the infield and the third set of five is the batters. As soon as the hitting group makes three outs, they move to the outfield, the outfield to the infield, and the infield becomes the hitters. Softball rules apply unless ground rules are established.

Three Person

There are four teams of three players each. One team of three begins play as the outfielders; another set plays at third, short, and second; a third set takes the positions of first, pitcher, and catcher; and the final set becomes the batting team. Ground rules can be devised for the specific situations. Rotate from batting to the outfield, outfield to the left side of the infield, the left side to the right side, and the right side moves in to bat.

Batter's Choice

Have "regular" teams except the teacher or a highly skilled player pitches for both teams. Each batter calls out the pitch he would like to hit—high, low, inside, outside, down the middle. The same pitch cannot be requested twice in one game. A maximum of two pitches is given to each batter. If the ball does not travel through the requested zone, it is called a ball. Two balls constitute a walk. If the batter swings and misses, hits a foul, or "takes" a ball that passes through the requested zone, a strike is called. Two strikes and the batter is out. The catcher is plate umpire. Official rules can apply or ground rules can be devised, example, six outs in a half inning or no stealing.

T-Ball

The game is played with all the players of the game; however, the pitcher does not pitch but the batters hit the ball off a batting tee. The batting tee must be moved out of the way when runners are coming home.

Co-ed Softball

Place an equal number, five and five in slow pitch and five and four in fast pitch, of male and female players on a team. Establish a male-female alternate batting order. Require the outfielders to play a specified distance from home, a minimum of 150 feet, when weaker hitting batters are at the plate. The outfielders cannot enter this "no man's zone" until after the ball is hit. Having the hitting team supply the pitcher for the defense, as in one pitch softball, and limit the number of pitches to two or three. If the female players are inexperienced, assign them to positions on the right side of the diamond where they will have to make relatively short throws to first base and receive fewer hard hit balls.

Glossary of Softball Terms

Appeal Play — A play upon which an umpire cannot make a decision until requested to do so by a player or coach.

Assist — A player receives fielding credit for helping a teammate make a putout.

At Bat — A player assumes the position in the batter's box. (One is not officially recorded as a time at bat if he walks, reaches base as a result of being hit by a pitched ball, or sacrifices.)

Away — The number of outs by the team at bat.

Ball — A pitch, call by the umpire, that does not travel through the strike zone and is not struck at by the batter or there is an illegal pitch.

*Balk — The pitcher makes a movement to pitch but does not immediately release the ball.

Base Hit — The scorer gives credit to the batter for reaching base because of the ball being hit and not because the defense miscues.

Battery — The pitcher and the catcher.

Batting Average — The player's batting percentage based upon the number of hits divided by the number of times at bat.

Batting Order — The official listing of a team's players in the order in which the members of that team must come to bat.

Backstop — A "nickname" for the catcher. The frame enclosure behind home plate.

Bag — The base.

Beat Out — The batter reaches base by running fast after hitting a slow moving ball and "beats" the throw.

Blocked Ball — A batted or thrown ball that is touched or stopped by a person not engaged in the game or that touched an object that is not part of the official equipment or playing area.

Blooper — A batted ball that arches just over the head of the infielders and just in front of the outfielders.

Bobble — The player juggles the ball while attempting to field it.

Bottom Half of the Inning — The team that took the field first is at bat.

Box — The batter's area, the catcher's area, the coaches' areas—all described and regulated by rules.

*Refers to the fast pitch game rules.

Box Score	A description of the game that is condensed by the use of symbols by scorekeepers who sit in the scorer's box.
*Bunt	A batted ball not swung at but intentionally met with the bat in such a way as to tap the ball slowly to the infield.
Change of Pace	The pitcher varies the speed of the pitched ball or varies the speed of ths pitching movements.
Circuit Clout	A home run.
Clean the Bases	The batter's hit allows all baserunners to score.
Clean-up Hitter	The number four batter in the batting order who is capable of "cleaning the bases" with a long hit.
Count	The number of balls and strikes on the batter.
Crowd the Plate	The batter stands very close to the plate by standing in the front edge of the box and/or leaning over the home plate.
Cut	A swing at a pitched ball.
Cut-off	A player intercepts a throw coming in, usually from the outfield, for the purpose of throwing out a runner other than the lead runner.
Diamond	The playing field formed by the four bases.
Double	A two-base hit.
Double Play	The two outs made on one play are a result of continuous action, usually resulting from a batted ball.
*Double Steal	The two baserunners steal on the same play.
Dead Ball	The ball is not in play and action ceases.
Down	The number of outs. The same as away.
Error	A misplay by a defensive player that results in batter or baserunner being safe at a base.
Earned Run	A run scored by proper play by the offense rather than because of an error by the defense.
Fair Ball	A batted ball that stops or is touched in fair territory between home and first base or home and third base; touches first, second, or third base; or lands in or is touched in fair territory in ths outfield; or passes out of the playing field while in fair territory.
Fan	The batter strikes out. The name given to a spectator.

*Refers to the fast pitch game rules.

Fielding Average	The player's fielding percentage based upon the number of errors made divided by the number of fielding chances one had.
Fielders Choice	The batter is safe because the defensive player chose to put out a preceding base runner.
Force Out	The out is a result of the defensive player in possession of the ball touching the base to put out the runner because the runner must move to that base.
Foul Ball	A batted ball that travels outside fair territory. (See fair ball.)
Foul Tip	A batted ball that goes directly into the hands of the catcher and is caught.
Fungo Hit	The ball is tossed in the air and batted by the tosser when hitting infield and/or outfield practice.
Fumble	A defensive player does not field the ball cleanly.
Full Count	The batter has three balls and two strikes.
Grand Slam	The batter hits a home run with the bases loaded.
Groove	The "heart" of the strike zone.
Grounder	A batted ball that travels to a fielder after bouncing on the ground soon after it leaves the bat.
Ground Rules	The local rules made to fit a specific situation.
*Hit Batsman	The batter is hit by a pitched ball and is awarded first base.
Hit and Run	An offensive play in which the base runner knows that the batter will attempt to hit the next pitch and begins to run as quickly as the rules permit. In fast pitch, it is as soon as the ball leaves the pitcher's hand and in slow pitch, it is as soon as the ball crosses home plate or is hit.
Hit the Dirt	The batter falls away from the plate to avoid being hit by a fast pitch. The runner is told to slide.
Hole	The area not covered by a defensive player. The space between players.
Hot Corner	The third base area.
Hot Box	The area between two bases in which a runner is caught and is being chased by the fielders in an attempt to make a put out (same as a run-down).
Home Run	A four base hit.
Infield	The area of the field normally covered by infielders in defensive positions.

*Refers to the fast pitch game rules.

Inning	The division of the game in which each team has had a turn at bat and a turn in the field; six outs.
Infield Fly	A fairly hit fly ball that in the opinion of the umpire should be caught by an infielder with ordinary effort. The batter is automatically out if there are less than two outs and there are runners on first and second bases, or first, second, and third bases.
Interference	A defensive player prevents or hinders a batter from hitting the ball or the offensive player impedes, hinders, or confuses a player while attempting to execute a play.
Keystone Sack	The second base area.
***Lay One Down**	A bunt.
Line Drive	A batted ball that travels in the air with a low trajectory sharply and directly off the bat.
No Hitter	The defense does not allow the opposing players to get a hit during a game; the official credit goes to the pitcher.
On Deck	The place where the next batter awaits his turn to bat.
Obstruction	A fielder who does not have the ball or is actively fielding a batted ball hinders the progress of a baserunner.
Outfield	The area of the field outside the diamond formed by the baselines or the area not normally covered by the infield and within the foul lines beyond first and third bases.
Overthrow	A play in which the ball, thrown from one fielder to another to retire a runner, goes into foul territory beyond the fielder attempting to catch the ball.
Over Run	To run past or beyond a base or overslide a base.
Pass	The batter is intentionally walked.
Passed Ball	A pitched ball is not handled properly by the catcher and gets away. The error is charged to the catcher.
Perfect Game	The defense allows no batter to reach base; Official credit goes to the pitcher.
Pickoff	A runner is trapped off the base by throwing behind the runner.
Pinchhitter	A stronger or better place hitter bats for another player.

*Refers to the fast pitch game rules.

*Pitch Out	A pitch is purposely thrown away from the batter so he cannot hit it and the catcher will have a chance to throw out a runner who may be stealing.
Play Ball	The umpire's verbal signal to put the ball into play.
Pop Up	A hit fly within or near the infield.
Pull Hitter	The batter meets the ball out in front to make it go down the left side of the field if batting righthanded, the right side of the field if lefthanded.
Put Out	The batter or base runner is not allowed to reach the base safely.
Rubber	The pitcher's plate.
Run Down	The runner is trapped between bases and is "run down" to be put out. (The same as hot box.)
Run	A score made by crossing home plate legally.
*Running Squeeze	The runner on third starts home as soon as the ball leaves the pitcher's hand because he knows that the batter will bunt.
RBI	The "run batted in" is made by batters whose hit brings a runner in to score.
Retire	The offensive player is put out.
Sacrifice Bunt	The baserunner advances to the next base because the defense has to make the play on the batter.
Sacrifice Fly	The baserunner scores after the defensive player has retired the batter by catching a fly ball.
*Safety Squeeze	The runner on third knows that the batter will bunt but does not break for home until the ball is bunted.
Scratch Hit	To get a hit even though the ball was hit weakly.
Shoestring Catch	A difficult catch of a sinking fly ball or line drive made just off the fielder's shoe tops.
Single	The batter reaches first base safely on a hit.
Slide	The runner, without slowing momentum, goes onto a base, feet or head first, in the dirt in an attempt to avoid being tagged.
Southpaw	A lefthanded player.
*Stealing	The baserunner attempts to advance to the next base during a pitch to the batter.
Step in the Bucket	The batter in attempting to hit the ball steps away from the plate and not forward with the foot nearest the pitcher.
Strike	The batter swings at a legally pitched ball and misses

*Refers to the fast pitch game rules.

or hits it foul. The umpire calls a strike if a legally pitched ball is in the strike zone but is not swung at by the batter.

Strike Out	The batter has three strikes.
*Strike Zone	The space over any part of the plate between the batter's arm pits and the tops of the knees when the natural batting stance is taken.
Strike Zone	The space over any part of the plate between the batter's highest shoulder and knees when the natural batting stance is taken.
Straight Away Hitter	The batter hits the ball straight ahead, through the middle of the field.
*Suicide Squeeze	The same as a running squeeze.
Texas leaguer	A fly ball that drops safely between the infielders and the outfielders (same as blooper).
Tag	The runner touches the base. A runner is touched by the ball or glove holding the ball.
Time	The play is over and the umpire suspends play.
Triple	A three-base hit.
Triple Play	The three outs are made on one play as a result of continuous action, usually after a batted ball.
Walk	The batter is awarded first base after four balls have been called.
*Wild Pitch	A pitch that the catcher cannot handle; the error is charged to the pitcher.

*Refers to the fast pitch game rules.

Index